BODY IN ACTION

Sarah Key

BBC BOOKS

Published by BBC Books,
a division of BBC Enterprises Limited,
Woodlands, 80 Wood Lane, London W12 0TT

First published 1992

ISBN 0 563 36390 8

Designed by Grahame Dudley Associates

Anatomical illustrations by Marks Creative Consultants
Copyright © 1992 BBC Books

Exercise illustrations by Heather Strahan
Copyright © 1992 Transworld Publishers (Australia) Pty Limited

Set in Palatino by Phoenix Photosetting Ltd, Chatham
Printed and bound in Great Britain by Clays Ltd, St. Ives plc.
Cover printed by Clays Ltd, St. Ives plc.

Contents

Acknowledgements page vi

CHAPTER 1
The Perfect State – ▶ *page 1*

CHAPTER 2
The Imperfect State – ▶ *page 5*

CHAPTER 3
*What Happens to
the Joints? –* ▶ *page 11*

CHAPTER 4
*What Can You Do
About It? –* ▶ *page 16*

CHAPTER 5
The Low Back – ▶ *page 22*

CHAPTER 6
The Thoracic Spine – ▶ *page 45*

CHAPTER 7
The Neck – ▶ *page 61*

CHAPTER 8
The Shoulders – ▶ *page 78*

CHAPTER 9
The Elbows – ▶ *page 95*

CHAPTER 10
The Wrists – ▶ *page 104*

CHAPTER 11
The Hips – ▶ *page 116*

CHAPTER 12
The Knees – ▶ *page 131*

CHAPTER 13
The Ankles – ▶ *page 148*

CHAPTER 14
The Feet – ▶ *page 164*

The 30 Minute Daily Regime ▶ *177*

Index page 182

Acknowledgements

My indebtedness goes to L. A. KAPANDJI whose texts on the physiology of joints are a bible. He is not only the anatomist, he is the artist – and despite all that, he's a Frenchman.

And his translator, whose fluent use of idiomatic English is so rare in a textbook – to use expressions like 'on the other hand' when you are talking about feet is some feat. And to cap it all off, he's a Frenchman.

And my indebtedness goes to Joyce, my yoga teacher, who doesn't notice when I collapse in class.

Sarah S. Key
February 1992.

To my loved ones.

Chapter One

THE PERFECT STATE

The other day I was driving in the dawn along one of Sydney's forest-fringed outer highways. It was one of those leafy dappled mornings of high summer, with the occasional shaft of sunlight bursting through the greenery and making explosions of light wherever it landed. Through the middle, cleaving its way through the foliage, ran my highway; the dusky blue of the bitumen blending and becoming as one with the miasma of the pre-dawn forest. As I rounded a corner I came up behind a cyclist, meandering at his ease across the nearside lane of the roadway. I hung back, because his actions had a compelling quality of beauty to them; a languid mark of excellence which made me want to stay and watch rather than speed past. I kept my distance, watching transfixed as he acted out in front of me a perfect virtuoso performance of human co-ordinated movement.

He was one of those men at the peak of physical fitness; he had the casual confident swagger of one who is very sure of his own body capability; and he was taking a breather. He dawdled and dreamed, back-pedalling and free-wheeling while he soaked in some of the breathy calm of the early day. He held the handle bars loosely with his left hand and then, in one deft movement, he reached down with his other hand and unsnapped the water bottle from the diagonal bar of the bike frame. And then, with the same casual ease, with the gentle speed of a ballerina and with the accuracy of a marksman, he raised the water bottle high above his head and, tilting his face back, squeezed a steady stream of water down into his open mouth. All the time his legs slowly pumping, effortlessly pushing the pedals around.

I motored on and soon enough came out into the harsh silver glare of the morning sun, where there were no cool chasms of green to give shade to the memory. But even now, long after, my mind is etched with the indelible picture of the man in the forest; that tranquil image of pirouetting and wheeling. The control, the timing, the finesse, the relaxed abandon; every bit as impressive as the gymnast on the balance beam or the soccer player before the goal. And yet this man was lost in his own reverie, oblivious to the incidental beauty of the way he was moving. He had no idea of the unwitting quality of his performance, so breathlessly admired by this unknown observer. He had no idea that his actions were the quintessence of human motor skills. He was out in the forest to watch the day wakening and to get his endorphin fix from a bike-ride. And to him, his superior co-ordination skills were a simple by-product of his search for fitness. And yet, he has it all. This is the human body at its best – long before his actions become etched in stone, long before 'age' starts to nibble at the corners of prowess.

All of us can catch a glimpse of excellence like this if we take the time to look: snatches of it where we least expect to see it. Everyday minutiae, there to be celebrated. Beauty in motion it is called. It can be savoured by standing back and looking at anyone at the peak of human ability. It doesn't have to be the more obvious deliverers of excellence: the ballet dancer with her deliberately choreographed *pas de deux*; or the Olympic speed skater with his prowling feline grace. It could just as easily be the simple craft of a butcher, for example, as he wields his knife about him. Standing back like a conductor of a symphony orchestra, free-flowing and precise, he cuts swathes of ham off the bone. Or it might be the economy of movement of a professional window-cleaner; the twirl and the swirl as he cleans a plate-glass window with a couple of swipes – at its best perhaps one of the most superb examples of beauty in economy of motion that you will ever see.

The human body is a sublime piece of machinery: towering over its narrow base, doing all manner of activities and hardly ever toppling over. It has it all, if we take the time to look. But it is the musculo-skeletal system, the co-ordinated system of muscles, joints and levers which puts our bodies into flight. We can watch our very own human frames act out the performance of fluent muscle effort because we have it too. Sliding and gliding through space in a symphony of synergic motion. And yet, we have no knowledge of the machinery which underlies this sublimely unselfconscious movement. No knowledge of the interplay of the dynamic systems which make these everyday movements so effortless for us. They just seem to happen as a commonplace part of everyday life, with all of us assuming they will go on by dint of right.

Looking at humans performing at the peak of fitness illustrates all too clearly what most of us have come to lack – and this is what this book is about. How our skeletal performance can drop so far below par that we simply shrug at the possibility of turning things around for the better. Function may have gone so far awry that you have acquired the companion of pain: not necessarily the raging tortured pains of broken bones, blood, gore and trauma but the aches and pains of a more subtle kind. Those petty afflictions, those nuisance grumblings from our bodies which slow us all down rather than stop us dead.

These are not serious; they are just the result of subtle breakdown of the joints – a whole bevy of afflictions which command scant regard within general medical practice but which are a nuisance none the less. They are what the medicos call 'musculo-skeletal disorders' as they dispatch us with pills and idle reassurances about 'time' and 'rest'. Those unsexy disorders which come on as we get older – tennis elbow, frozen shoulder, arthritis of the hip, cartilage

3

trouble, lumbago, repetitive strain injury and so on. Skeletally speaking, the end of the road for the joint; the final pictures of acute discomfort in a slowly evolving story, when all the way along the route there were increasingly obvious tell-tale signs of crotchetiness and a stiff skeleton making all the creaks and groans of a distinctly labouring machine.

But, as well as these physical signs of a system seizing up, there is the cosmetic side; where we are concerned not with pain but with premature ageing. That insidious mantle, that cloak, that invisible skein of debility which descends upon us all and claims us – if we let it – into the territory of the 'early aged'.

This book is for and about 'Joe Average'. Not my cyclist in the forest and not Bjorn Borg. You, the one who admires the antics of Centre Court but who feels excluded by their excellence. It's you in the middle I'm interested in; you who I want to bring on. I want you to 'do something' at the very least to thwart the settling of age and, at the more ambitious, to deal successfully with unwelcome aches and pains.

Chapter Two

THE IMPERFECT STATE

The human skeleton is a supremely competent structure. It is very tall, very strong, very agile, and able to do an extra-ordinary variety of things. It stands there high above the ground and is kept upright and functioning usefully by our superior neuro-muscular control. This means that at one level our brain tells us what to do but at a lower level the brain instructs our postural muscles simply to keep us upright, so that we can do all those other useful things. I say 'simply' but really it isn't simple at all; it is a feat of insuperable grandeur. It is only that in comparison with other complex acts such as playing a cello (let alone reading the score), it is a simple act to stay upright.

But we can get it wrong and the skeleton does go wrong. We encumber the postural mechanism which keeps us upright with an unduly heavy yoke of lassitude and bad habits, so that we develop a list as we stand there. We lose that dynamic uprightness; we bend and bow in all the wrong places. The skeleton resembles a ship's mast. As we stand there tall, we are kept straight by a collection of forward, aft and lateral stays which keep the mast balanced. In humans, the stays are the muscular system which works on the levers and keeps the bones straight. But the human frame is slightly more complicated than a ship's mast. It is divided into segments for a start, with each of those segments able to move independently of the other. So it is hard to keep the human mast straight, especially when perpetual habits of poor posture and movement cause the muscular stays to become unequal in length and strength. The mast develops a bow.

This comes about for several reasons. The foremost is that most of the 'doing', most of the actions of precision function of the human body take place in a flexed or hunched-over posture. We do this so that we can focus our eyes on the task at hand but the result is that over time we develop a subtle 'lean' and the skeleton loses its dynamic balance. It may not be all that obvious; you might not look bowed as you stand there (although some people do). It's just that you find you can touch your toes easily enough but when it comes to bending backwards the other way you can barely get beyond vertical. This is the first flaw; the critical flaw. And it is this which sets the stage for 'difficulty' for all the other lesser joints. Wherever they might be – the jaw, the knee, or perhaps the big toe – if they are off balance they don't run as well. If mother skeleton fails to stand upright, then all the other joints become slightly more hampered in their individual action. A simple parallel though perhaps a fanciful one: if a skyscraper stands at an angle in the sky then all the internal machinery works at a disadvantage: the elevators don't run smoothly up and down the lift shafts, the doors and windows don't close properly, the desks inch across the floors . . . just as well the leaning tower at Pisa doesn't have elevators. The truism is that the better the joints run, the better we run.

The next factor which encourages our curled-over stance is the general dearth of variety in the way we use our bodies. Not only do we tend to do all our activities bent; we don't do anything much else. We tend to do the same sorts of things in the same sorts of ways, at the same sorts of times, for ever and a day. Creatures of habit, we even get up at about the same hour every morning. We make the same movement to get out of bed (perhaps the most taxing activity of the day), we bend over the basin, we put our foot on a stool to do up our shoelaces, we turn the key in the front door. And invariably the whole day runs on as a collection of unvarying physical habits. Our workbenches are all at the optimal height; we don't even put our hand out of the car window to make a signal – the indicator lever is only a few centimetres from the steering wheel. Variety is the exception rather than the rule and this meagreness of variety leads us to trouble.

We could compensate for the usual flexed postures of precision work if we did more 'antidote actions' to balance the time spent crumpled. But we don't. At the end of a day we sit hunched-up and deep in a sofa. We get up and mooch across the room; a complete absence of romp, no verve, no spring, no flamboyance, no joy . . . no variety in the way we move. After a taxing period spent bent over reading the paper, we rarely arch backwards, we rarely extend our spines and take our arms up behind the head and stretch. We remain locked in by our stereotyped patterns of behaviour and our joints become trapped by our own habits.

This lack of imagination, this lack of flourish, means that the role of our joints is steadily reduced to the slimmest repertoire of function: those same old movements time after time – the hand to your mouth but rarely behind your back. The legs back and forth at the hips as you walk but rarely the knees up under your chin, and never the splits. Like the old-wives' tale of our wide-eyed childhood, the wind has changed and made permanent the grimaces; only this time it is not the face but the joints. The joints crimp. All of them. They lose the ability to move into areas where they hardly ever go. If the freedom is not needed the soft tissues shrink, and sooner rather than later, the joints lose the capacity to go there, even if they wanted to. Joint action loses opportunity, loses variety. It loses lubrication, elastic stretch, even its clothing of muscle tissue. Joint action dries up. Pain is but a whisker away.

So the root cause of joint problems is a lack of variety in the *way* we use our bodies. That's the nuts and bolts of it. But what adds insult to this chronic state of unpreparedness is the next set of factors:

7

repetition or the overuse of the movements that we do make. This also brings trouble. It seems that we either do too little or too much, that we alternate between indolence on the one hand and over-activity on the other. A very bad combination. Sport is usually the offender here but so too is the occasional bout of activity in the desert of non-activity: that sudden leaping up from the sofa and doing a spate of shovelling in the garden. The skeleton struggles to accommodate the quantum leap from the meagreness of non-activity to repetitive aggressive activity. Maybe it is because the skeleton *seems* to cope uncomplainingly so often that we assume that it will go on coping . . . indefinitely.

Any smooth-running joint will be thrown by being the victim of one dominant muscle group. It will be wrenched and yanked in a subtle repetitive way. This happens particularly in sports such as tennis or golf which consist of regimentally defined patterns of movement. The serve in tennis demands absolutely rigid adherence to the same pattern, over and over again. Your aim is to ace your opponent by making as precise a movement as possible. At least in tennis there is the backhand and a limited range of forehand strokes but this is not the case with golf. Golf just requires the same swing, in the same direction, with as much clout as you can muster. Not good. Imagine what it does to your skeleton: nothing immediately disastrous and nothing that cannot be undone with some attention but it sets up a whispering discord in various joints, which the skeleton then has to struggle to smooth over.

It is bad enough to have a skeleton which stands there bowing in space with the shoulders forward and the belly protruding but it is even worse to have that skeleton beset by a patchy scatter of miscell-aneous muscle groups, some of which are stronger and tighter than the rest. The bowing of the skeleton is brought about by poor static postures; going back to the analogy of the ship's mast, the front stays are too tight and the back stays too weak. A more accurate analogy would be a puppet. A puppet has a hard job functioning well if there are some strings which pull easily and others which don't; where some strings are too tight, others too loose. The result is discord: clonking subtle discord. What is true of the puppet is also true of the skeleton.

Balance of muscular control is the very essence of healthy movement. All joints are human hinges which permit movement between one bone and the next. In the perfect state, they form a marvellously dynamic perfectly poised system. They bend and straighten with effortlessly gliding movement. The degree of bend and the speed at which that movement takes place is under the control of the muscles. The important point is that for every muscle performing a set movement there is always its counter-partner to perform the reverse movement. For friction-free action both need to be well-matched in length and in strength. Take the knee for example: the hamstrings bend the knee, the quadriceps at the front of the thigh straighten it. If both groups are equally balanced the knee can be nursed through the most extravagant explosions of movement. If they are not well-paired the knee can easily suffer, even with the most paltry exertions. If, for example, the hamstrings are tight and do not allow the knee to straighten fully and, at the same time, the thigh muscles are weak and unable to match the hamstrings in their obstinacy, it is an easy thing to tweak the knee. You might find that you were just turning on the field and you went down. Not even tackled. But it can happen just as easily in the aisle of a supermarket: just turning to pick up the marmalade and down you go.

When we are young, or even in later life if we are particularly lithe and skeletally well-balanced, the body does not hurt itself easily like this. Then our skeleton is covered with well-paired muscle groups and all the joints display a fine elastic quality: the springiness that the young Romanian gymnast of yesteryear demonstrated to a superlative degree. Muscles and joints can perform at their best: they can act powerfully and they are also powerful absorbers of shock. But as we get older, repetitive and stereotyped movements will upset this balance. A joint will be 'pinched' by being in the grip of one dominant muscle in the pair. This takes time to manifest itself but sooner or later the running of the joint will start to get out of kilter. Insidious chafing and knocking will start. In a nutshell, the incompetent muscle balance exposes the joint to phenomenal wear and tear.

You might not realise it in the early stages. You are unaware that a joint is starting to run hot from the subtle grind it suffers when it fails to run true. You may only realise it somewhere down the track when debility or even pain starts to creep in. It dawns on you that the odd movement is painful; a pain over your forearm when you shake hands, a pain in your upper arm when you put on your coat, or a tightness in one knee when you squat on your haunches.

It is possible that you might recognise that something is wrong before the pain and severe disability creeps in, if you have your wits about you. You might notice that one arm is failing to go as high up above your head as the other or that your knees are starting to click and grate whenever you bend over. But these changes are mostly creeping in their stealth. You will probably have been unaware of what was happening. At the most you felt a twinge: you thought 'I mustn't do that any more', and you passively gave way to age.

Chapter Three

WHAT HAPPENS TO THE JOINTS?

Let's assume that you are like me, the more commonplace specimen of humanity. We're the ones who catch sight of ourselves in glass shopfronts and are momentarily appalled by what we see. We have suffered from the weight of time. We are the ones developing a crook in the back, bottom sticking out like a boomerang. Or is it our shoulders that droop or our head carried too far forwards, in front of the line of our body? Or do our knees bend but won't fully straighten? Whatever they are, these are all the tell-tale signs of age. Our skeletons have become blighted as if by a wand, and suddenly we recognise the yoke of time.

The ultimate result of less than perfect muscle control is escalating loss of what is known as accessory joint movement or joint play. Joint play is best described as the intangible 'extra' movements of a joint. They are movements between bones which exist but cannot be seen by the naked eye; those subtle gliding accommodating movements which give a joint an extra adaptability, an innate ability to absorb shock, an innate sense of being young.

A wrist is a good joint to demonstrate accessory movement. The wrist is not a simple hinge. It is made up of a complex of eight small bones which articulate between themselves and then between the bottom of the radius, one of the two bones of the forearm. All the time, whatever the wrist or hand movement, there is a shuffling harmonious interplay between these small bones so that the inside of the wrist resembles a bag of moving bones. At any point you would be hard put to say what any one bone is doing but each is doing its own thing. Rather like loose ice-cubes floating within a bag, every bone moves in concert but independently, to give the wrist that astonishing 360-degree freedom at the bottom of the forearm.

The wrist is an overt example of accessory movement. A more subtle example is the knee which at face value seems to have only one movement. You might think that the knee is just a hinge which bends and straightens but you would be wrong. For the knee to function optimally, it must have its full component of internal manoeuvrability. It must be able to angle a bit, left and right, and also to glide a bit, backwards and forwards, mostly to cater for irregularities in walking surfaces. But more importantly the knee must have a subtle but valuable essence of twist, to bring about the complex act of locking the leg so that we can stand on it. This will be discussed in greater detail in the chapter on knees. But even from this brief description it will be plain to you how unplain the accessory twist of the knee is.

Loss of accessory movement can wreak all manner of havoc upon a joint. At best, the loss simply disadvantages the superlative function of the joint. At worst you have crippling pain. If you only suffer minor losses of accessory movement, the joint simply loses that ultimate dimension of its quality function; that zenith of operating ability which keeps it in the realms of the perfect state. It loses its quintessence of versatility. It loses its enhanced accuracy and its ease of performance. It loses its ability to line up for that optimal angle of action. In other words, it has lost its intangible quality of youth. To the senses, it has lost that 'forgiving' feel. It thuds rather than floats on air. And this is the way we all get older. The subtle background movements are the first to disappear. We may not know it but under the skin the laxity is ebbing away and the joint is losing its play.

Of course, the ageing process has an inevitable role to play. Whatever we do or don't do, the tissues do age. This is a physiological truism. The older we get, the less elastic our tissues become. We lose our 'elastin' content and increase on 'fibrin'. This means that they lose stretch. Just as the skin around our eyes becomes wrinkled and crepey, alas!, so do the tissues around the joints. The joints lose their bounce. They become thicker in appearance, less elastic and dry. And as the joints lose their romp, they become squeezed of their accessory movement. Their internal manoeuverability is choked.

Even before we get old, the process can be speeded up by poor muscle control which puts strain on the joints. Muscle irresponsibility stirs the pot in the mixture of advancing years and hard work. Again, using the analogy of the ship's mast, the mast manages to stay up while the boat floats over mirrored glassy waters. But when the going gets rough and the lurching boat is buffeted by the waves, the strain tells. Unlike the human joint, the mast will eventually snap. And the joint? The joint is a little more enduring but will suffer if exposed to profound increases in wear and tear.

At this point, it is important to explain exactly how it is that imperfect muscle control speeds up the loss of accessory joint freedom. It is the result of the reaction in tissues which are subject to irritation. Imagine an elbow as victim to poor muscle parity. It works like a double pulley with ropes pulling back and forth through it. If one rope is shorter it will chafe as it pulls through. Friction is set up between the muscles working in close-knit harmony around the joint. Inflammation is the result, with one struggling tendon less comfortable in action by the minute. As it becomes inflamed it loses its capacity to accept stretch. It refuses to join in normal activity because stretch hurts. We unwittingly indulge the whim and relinquish an increment of joint freedom.

This is how it starts. And this is how it goes on. A muscle chafes, gets inflamed, declines to stretch – and a whisker of joint performance closes down. This is the acute stage you might not even know about it. You may just register a sore arm for a day or so, after some painting perhaps, but it goes away. You spare the joint from doing things it doesn't like – you lay off painting the ceiling. In time everything settles. The angriness of the short-lived acute episode subsides and the chronic picture takes over. Inflammation soothes, swelling disperses and normality reigns. Only there's the rub; things are not quite normal again. Not quite all the freedom returns. As the cloud of noxious irritation lifts, it unveils a joint which has some compartments still closed down. And having gained a quiet life they are loathe to give it up. Try to push the joint where it doesn't want to go and it won't like it.

At this point we do one of two things. Either we stay as we are and don't ask the joint to do things it doesn't want to do, letting it hang on to its new tight inactive ways. Or we barge through. We make the joint participate in normal activity. This can also go one of two ways. We may do just enough measured movement to coax the tight components back into full and useful function or we may go over the limit and provoke the joint into a nasty angry reaction.

This explains why sometimes activity is the right thing to do for a joint, and sometimes it is not. Why sometimes going for a run on a sore ankle is just what it needs but sometimes you come back hobbling. It is all to do with the degree of resistance, and getting it right in how much you push it. Too much too fast and the joint will clam up.

This also explains how it is that you can keep on injuring a joint; injuring and re-injuring and re-injuring it. If its performance has fallen so far below par all actions will amount to trauma. Anything will hurt it. The joint is so tight that it can barely accommodate any function at all. This is common with ankles: an initial nasty wrench then a second twist a couple of weeks later in another fluke accident. Thereafter the ankle is never the same again. You are always going over on it. Always easy to hurt; an accident waiting to happen.

Trouble escalates when the muscles around the injured joint lock tight (protective spasm). This is an automatic response activated when the brain senses a joint is hurt. In the case of the ankle, the muscles around the ankle go so stiff that it cannot bend or straighten and you are forced to walk with a limp.

You may not remember when you first injured a joint. You could have hurt it but easily passed it off. You may have done something ten years ago, or was it fifteen? You might not have been aware that one joint was not the equal of the other. On the other hand, you might have wondered why it is that you keep hurting one ankle but never the other. What you didn't know was that the muscle clench had become ever-present, trimming the joint on all sides. More and more avenues of accessory joint movement had closed down. The ankle was becoming stiffer in more and more of its movements, setting itself up to be more and more easily hurt.

This is the common picture leading up to joint injury: stealthy loss of accessory freedom. It also explains why trivial incidents can amount to major injury. 'I hardly did anything and the ankle went.' The truth was you had it coming to you. You had a joint which was subtly and increasingly being flawed by loss of accessory freedom until it reached the point where any injury was going to amount to a catastrophe.

In a broader sense, this can be happening to all the joints around your body if you have widespread poor muscle co-ordination. And this is how the skeleton gradually locks down. One by one, each joint will lose its floppy joint play and tighten up. Their major functions will be there; your knee will still bend and straighten well enough but it will have an increasingly reduced margin of adaptability. These are the joints which attract further injury. This is how the skeleton wears out.

Chapter Four

WHAT CAN YOU DO ABOUT IT?

After all this bad news, you must be wondering what can be done about it. Well, the good news is that there is lots to be done. No matter how badly you have used your body, however improperly paired your muscle groups have become you *can* reverse the trends that are happening at your joints. Joints can be unkinked. It is not as difficult as you might think and you can do it yourself.

Each particular joint has its own sequence it will follow when it comes to losing mobility. It will kink in its own predestined pattern; a shoulder will lose its ability to let the arm roll up and out as it goes up above your head, a knee to swivel and fully straighten. As different as we all are in our body build – our habits, our weight, our fitness, our jobs or our leisure – each joint will go the same way. And it doesn't matter whether you are a high-jumper, a farmer or an office worker. Every joint, when it starts to go, will follow that joint's pattern and lose the same movements first.

Yoga has all the answers. Whoever the original yogis were, they certainly knew what they were on about. They knew the ways joints tighten; which movements 'old' joints find hard to do. Accordingly, there is a complete range of yoga procedures which can be harvested for what they can do to rejuvenate each joint of the skeleton.

But yoga seems to have a bad name. It seems to be associated with occult ceremonies of incense burning and people standing on their head. To my mind, there are few things cleverer than yoga: not only the stretches but in its broadest sense; the discipline, the meditation, the breathing, the elevated states of mental awareness and so on. Perhaps not all these avenues are readily accessible to the hurried habits of Western man but each of us has something to gain.

The supreme gift of yoga is its physical prowess; quite simply, its ability to restore accessory movement to the joints. The fruits are plucked along the way, on the journey, not at the destination. This simple tenet, so readily misunderstood by the dismissive band of doubters, is what turns people away from yoga in droves. These are the people who say: 'It hurt too much so I didn't think I should do it,' or, 'I've never been able to touch my toes, so why start now?'. But yoga is the most simple and effective way of keeping the joints apart; of keeping them young. There is no great value in reaching the destination; no great value in reaching the toes (I tell myself this as I feel sorry for the people in my yoga class who can put their flat hands on the floor). The value lies in the process of getting there and this is where we Westerners often get it wrong. By concentrating upon point scoring, getting the goal, end-gaining for the sake of it, we fail to appreciate the subtlety of our bodies opening out en route; the little improvements along the way, of feeling freer, feeling lighter, the feeling of our bodies getting younger.

I believe suppleness is much overlooked in today's pursuit of strength and aerobic fitness but it is suppleness that you want – or at least need. Stretch. Releasing the skeleton. Unhitching it and taking it out of the confines of its habitual kinks and bends. And the two are as different as night and day. Aerobics is the equivalent of the quick fix. You feel better for it because of the oxygen flush-out, rather as you do after a run, a cycle, a swim, or a game of squash, golf or tennis. But doing aerobics without undoing the ill-effects of aggressive muscle work is to achieve a very lopsided victory. And

17

reinforcing one set of sporting patterns on top of your routine habits of movement, often means that sport becomes your Waterloo.

Perhaps it is a deviant 'healthy' offshoot of the punitive work ethic that leads many of us to see value in the perverse pleasure of dripping sweat and racing pulse. The very fact that yoga takes time is the principal factor in turning people away; as if the qualities of calmness and deliberate anti-haste are in some way going to attach themselves to the working habit and rob us of vital reserves of power and punch we need in our working lives.

Yoga is not like that. It is pedantic and exacting, and the aim is to do it calmly and well and to the extreme. Near enough is not good enough. It takes years to become an expert (Mr Iyengar, the founder of the Iyengar School of Yoga in India claims today, after practising yoga for some sixty years, that he is just a beginner). Yoga consists of a series of unyielding edicts through exacting physical postures. The battle is with yourself not some clock on the wall or some pile of weights on a machine. You need good breathing control to make the hard things easier and at times it requires immense willpower to maintain a lip-bitingly difficult posture. It also has to be said that many of the postures hurt.

I make it sound depressing; I make it sound as if all other forms of physical exercise are weak and meretricious by contrast. I don't mean to (or do I?). I simply mean to extol the virtues of a subtle discipline and explain its benefits for the wider realm of health.

Yoga helps us all. By and large, whether we are a rice grower in the provinces of China or an Inuit from Greenland, we all tend to use our bodies in similar ways. We Westerners are a little worse off because the mod-cons in our lives have wiped out much of the variety in the way we do things. But even so, arms do arm things, and backs do back things, and so on. For each specific part of the body, there is a specific variety of actions which predominate. This leads to the joints developing a penchant for only doing their main action, while letting their other lesser actions lapse. And we all kink in the same way.

So, it is not a single action which causes tight joints but a repeating pattern. The superiority of yoga is that it knows this. None of the postures will reinforce the habitual actions of the joints and all of them will reintroduce forgotten territory. Unlike other more facile forms of body-stretching, it will undo the pattern rather than a single movement. This is the shortfall of so many of the gymnasium regimes, with their hasty stretches at the end of a gym circuit or weight-training programme. There, scant regard is paid to undoing the pattern of the sporting action; they use simple stretches rather than complex.

That leads me to the final plus of the gentle art of yoga: the staggeringly rich variety in the choice of the stretches. You can start off with the most modest disarmingly gentle stuff, where you really find it hard to believe that anything is happening at all, and then eventually progress to the almost impossible. You can start at any level and progress at any rate. This highlights another difference between yoga and other forms of exercise. In a normal gym class, you go in at the level the class is already at – sometimes with devastating results, as I know from my own clinical experience.

Yoga does take time and effort. Sometimes it is agony just to hold a stretch for a matter of seconds. But this is what it is all about. The more it hurts, the more you need it. In time all the soft tissues are loosened, even the blood vessels and the nerves, as the body is reintroduced to its extremes. Elasticity is restored and so is stream-lined smooth-gliding function. The stretches pull the tissues and create a much more vigorous blood supply. Blood rushes to the tissues to mop up after the unexpected demands on flexibility and the circulation through the tissues changes from a torpor to a flush. The skeleton is cleansed and rejuvenated.

At the end of each of the following ten chapters you will find a series of yoga exercises to help you restore full mobility to your joints. Follow them carefully and slowly. It is better to do just a few exercises properly than rush through the whole set badly.

If you start off knowing you already have a problem joint, be prepared to take things slowly. At the start, it may be impossible to progress beyond the first exercise. Even then you may feel you are doing it so badly it is hardly worth continuing. But don't give up. There is nothing wrong with staying on the first exercise for weeks if you have to. And don't worry if your efforts look nothing like the illustrations. It's all in the journey. Eventually you will get nearer to the way it looks in the book and the benefits are happening all along the way. In the early stages, you may not be able to hold the exercise for the length of time I suggest. If this happens, come out of the posture earlier, flop the limb or the part around to ease the discomfort (even massage it yourself for a bit) and then try it again. You can do this up to four times.

Do not be tempted, incidentally, to try strengthening a problem joint before you have restored its full function. Of course this flies in the face of conventional medical thinking which usually urges strengthening of problem joints as the universal panacea; flogging a dead horse; well nearly dead. Whether it is a shoulder that won't go up or a knee which won't straighten, it is futile to keep exercising it to get it strong. If you approach the problem from the other direction, that is to restore its accessory performance first, you will find that the strength comes back of its own accord with minimal need for exercising.

If you do not have a specific joint problem and just need a general body-toner regime, there is the 30 Minute Daily Regime on page 177. It deals with all the different parts of the body in turn. As you go through, it will be apparent to you which joints are the most resistant to stretch. These are the areas to concentrate on. You can then go to the chapter on that joint and do its entire exercise regime as a daily event. Each joint regime has been graded from the easiest to the most difficult but you should try them all. Even a few seconds of the hardest ones will bring results. Only in cases of severe dysfunction of a joint (discussed in each chapter under the heading 'Common Disorders') should you be content with doing only the first couple of exercises of the regime.

A suggestion for an overall programme is the 30 Minute Daily Regime as a body-toner, followed by the regime for one joint; a different joint every day. This will mean an hour's workout but it is a very effective system. You will find that you will quite quickly develop your favourite exercises, just as you will sense the ones that your body needs. Hopefully these will be one and the same.

If the stretches are being effective you should feel a permanent though minimal state of muscle soreness; all through the next day a sensation of mild but agreeable discomfort as if 'something is happening'. If it goes beyond this and it hurts all the time then you need to lay off a bit: a shorter length of time holding each exercise, no repetition and stopping short of the most demanding ones at the end of each regime. If the soreness takes more than a few days to dissipate then you should drop down to exercising twice or three times a week rather than daily. But do remember, in the overall scheme of things, soreness is no bad thing. With frank joint problems you will find the old familiar pain is replaced by a different sort of muscle tenderness. This is one of the best signs of progress.

As a rule it is better to do the stretching at the end of the day, ideally an hour or two after dinner before going to bed. We are always stiffer in the mornings and the spectre of the looming day makes it harder to relax your way through each exercise. Another good time is mid-morning when the house is quiet and there is no rush. It is never good to do the exercise regime on a full stomach.

You must take care to keep breathing evenly as you do each exercise. Resist the temptation to trap the breath as the full discomfort of each stretch becomes apparent. Don't tense the body and fight against your own muscles. As you go into each stretch, will yourself to relax. Concentrate on slow quiet breathing and let your head float away. You will feel the resistance of your body palpably melt as the relaxation takes effect. But as you near your limit of endurance your body will start to harden again, a sign that it is time to come out of the stretch. If you are over-tired or tense, you will reach your limit sooner. Listen to your body and watch for these subtle signs. Unclutter your mind and take your body slowly, and you will be there.

Chapter Five

THE

LOW BACK

What is the Low Back?

The lumbar spine is a flexible segmented pillar at the bottom of the torso and immediately above the sacrum; a chunky movable scaffolding to support the rest of the spine towering above it. The spinal column passes up through the back of the abdomen which balloons out in front of it. The heavy corseting of the abdominal muscles holds the abdominal wall in, reefed back close to the spine. But muscle weakness, common to most human beings, often allows the wall to sag and the abdominal contents to fall forwards.

The lumbar spine is made up of five lumbar vertebrae. The bottom one, number five, sits lashed on to the sloping surface of the top of the sacrum. The sacrum does not participate in spinal mobility. It is a fused amalgam of five sacral vertebrae with the vestigial tail, the coccyx, at the bottom. The sacrum forms the central strut at the back of the pelvis with the two big ear-shaped bones, called the ilia, joining the sacrum at either side at the sacro-iliac joints.

The lumbar vertebrae are built to bear weight. They are stacked around a gentle curve known as the lumbar lordosis which gives the

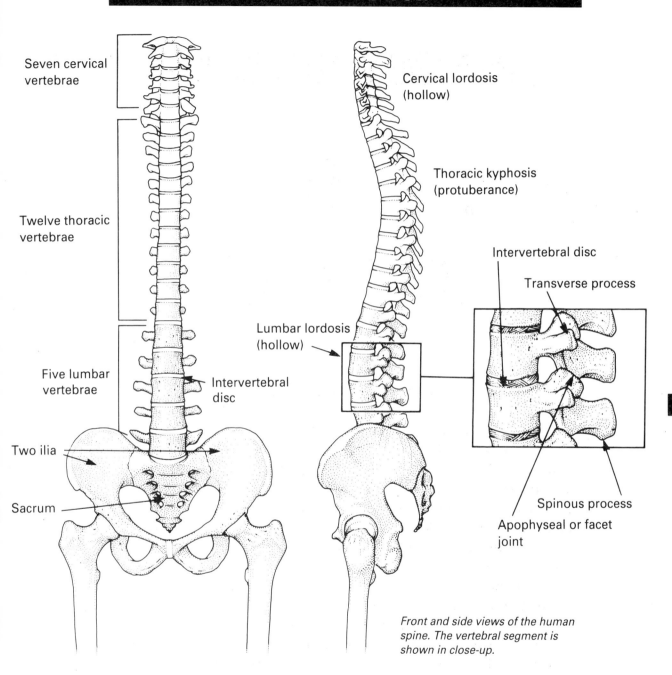

Seven cervical
vertebrae

Cervical lordosis
(hollow)

Twelve thoracic
vertebrae

Thoracic kyphosis
(protuberance)

Intervertebral disc

Transverse process

Lumbar lordosis
(hollow)

Five lumbar
vertebrae

Intervertebral
disc

Two ilia

Sacrum

Spinous process

Apophyseal or facet
joint

*Front and side views of the human
spine. The vertebral segment is
shown in close-up.*

low back a natural hollow when viewed from the side. The curve is
brought about by slight wedging of the front of each vertebra so that
the column bows forward, rather than sits straight. From the side
view each vertebra has a slight narrowing or waist-like appearance.

This helps it to bear weight, although most of its weight-bearing brilliance comes from its trabeculae, an internal three-dimensional grid of fine strands of bone.

Trabeculae have the appearance at first glance of a honeycomb mesh inside the cavity of the bone. But on closer scrutiny, you see a fine network of vertical pillars and horizontal struts. The vertical pillars prevent the bones impacting downwards and pulverising into bony rubble under the pressure of body weight. And the horizontal shoring prevents the bones caving in at the sides like a cardboard carton. All weight-bearing bones have them; they look like iron filings following lines of force, depending on where the weight is transmitted through the bone. It's an ingenious system which means that the bone does not have to be solid to provide strength – it can be light yet strong.

The intervertebral discs sit between all the vertebrae in the spine like squashy water-filled pillows, cushioning the bone to bone contact of one vertebra sitting on the next. They are thickest in the lumbar area and their presence gives the spine that sensational bounce romp and twist. In many ways a disc resembles a radial car

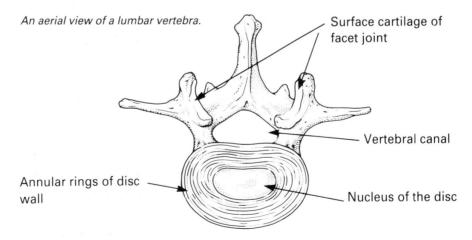

An aerial view of a lumbar vertebra.

Surface cartilage of facet joint

Vertebral canal

Annular rings of disc wall

Nucleus of the disc

tyre in that its walls are made up of layers of diagonal meshing, each successive layer lying at right angles to the one before. This gives fantastic strength to the walls and yet allows the vertebrae the freedom to twist and gap open when we move.

The walls of the disc also bear weight and are prevented from buckling in and collapsing by the radially 'squirting' pressure of the nucleus inside the disc. The nuclei behave like liquid ball bearings at the centre of their disc. There they all are, stacked vertically and rolling around on one another, so we can achieve that incredible willowy movement of the spine. The strength of the disc wall plays its part in keeping the nucleus contained. It is helped by an intrinsic quality of the nucleus: its ability to attract and hold water to itself. This keeps the disc plumped up and squashy so that it is resilient to shock, like a fully inflated car tyre.

Each vertebra joins centrally with its neighbour vertebrae through the vertebra-disc union, but it also makes bone to bone junctions at the bony ring at the back. As one vertebra sits on another, they make two bony notches at the back of the intervertebral disc, flanking the central hole which goes to make up the neural tube which houses the actual spinal cord. These bony notches are called the apophyseal or facet joints and, because of their bone to bone contact they are the first to suffer rub if the disc loses water content and deflates.

The facet joints are synovial joints like most other joints in the body. This means they are held together by a capsule and have their opposing cartilaginous surfaces washed and lubricated by a viscous fluid. Like all other synovial joints, they are easily strained and have a prompt response to that strain. Unlike the intervertebral disc, the facet joints have a highly sophisticated nervous network to keep us posted on their state of health. I believe that the facet joints are the most overlooked source of pain in the back, especially in the low back which is more subject to the squashing pressures of body weight. Here the facet joints frequently take the brunt of chronic vertical jamming, as well as the brunt of limiting the degree of twisting of the lower back.

The round brick part of the vertebra bears weight. Behind this is a circular arch or hole made by a ring of vertebral bone. When one vertebra is superimposed on the one below, each bony ring goes to make a continuous tube inside the vertebral column, running the entire length of the spine. It is in this bony tube that the precious and fragile vertebral cord is housed and from where it transacts its almost unintelligible electrical networking of nervous impulses from the brain to the periphery of the body.

At the level of each vertebral segment, two spinal nerves branch off the cord and pass out to the external body. They leave the column by running right beside the facet joint on one side and the intervertebral disc on the other. The nerve can therefore be easily irritated by the bulging proximity of an unhealthy disc wall or an inflamed facet joint. Either condition can cause pain in the leg, known as sciatica.

How Does the Low Back Work?

Very well if you ask me. The lumbar vertebrae are the bricks at the bottom of the stack; the stack being the beautifully designed upright human spine. The bones provide the stability, the intervertebral discs provide the shock absorption and the mobility and the facet joints provide the security. It is a solid and sturdy arrangement with the intervertebral discs sitting between the chunks of bone like dynamic hydro-elastic pillows, cushioning the impaction of the vertebra.

The spine acts as the dynamic internal scaffolding of the body. The fact that this tall apparatus possesses such a handsome repertoire of mobility is what makes the human spine almost incredible. Both the anatomy of the spine and the soft tissue system make this freedom possible. Several factors glue the spine together to stop it falling apart like a child's collapsing column of building blocks.

Perhaps the most important are the intervertebral discs. They provide dramatic positive cohesion between the spinal segments. The discs are tenaciously embedded to the flat upper and lower surfaces of the vertebrae between which they sit and when the spine bends over, the walls of the discs dampen the movement. As the vertebrae pull apart, the layers of meshed lattice making up the disc wall are stretched (rather like stretching a square of garden lattice); the further it goes, the greater the tension created in the mesh.

Bending forwards is the most grandiose of the lumbar spine's movement, and here another set of factors helps to control the unwieldiness of the action: the dynamic balance between the functions of the ligaments and the facet joint notching. Ligaments run up and down the spine, bandaging it together and binding it up tight. But even with the help of substantial muscle shoring the ligamentous system would fray in time. The soft tissue alone could not keep the spine from falling apart through a lifetime of bending.

The facet joints are the ultimate block to the spine coming undone. They are designed in such a way that the surface of the upper and lower vertebrae notch together and prevent shear. Like locking the hands together by cupping the fingertips over each other, each vertebra is prevented from slipping forwards or backwards off the one below. The mutual impediment of a bony catch keeps them snug. The facet joints hook the vertebrae together in a chain, with the tension kept on the column by the tension of the muscles and ligaments clothing the spine.

There is a 'slope' of the lower surface of the facet joint and this shape encourages greater tension from the ligamentous hold, the further we bend over. The more we bend forwards and the more the top vertebra moves forwards on the one below, the further it runs up the slope of the surface of the lower bone. This 'upwards' travel separates the vertebrae and so creates greater tension in the spinal ligaments. The more we bend over, the tighter our spine is; sprung together by its ligaments. Another simple but ingenious system.

Our own volitional input to spinal stability comes from the strength of the supporting abdominal wall; the tummy muscles. Strength of these, or lack of it, has the most major role to play in the welfare of our backs. In brief, if our tummy wall works well, our spines work well. The tummy muscles have two functions. First, they act like a forward retaining wall. By tightening when they contract, the muscles raise the intra-abdominal pressure which prevents too much forward shear of one vertebra off the one below.

Secondly, they have a more esoteric 'offloading' effect which works rather like this: if you grasp a plastic bottle full of water around its waist, the pressure of your hands on the side of the bottle will make water spurt out of the top of the bottle. A tight contraction of the tummy muscles will do the same with the contents of the abdomen. Tight tummy tone will hoist up the contents and offload their dragging pressure on the base of the spine.

You can see what a bonus strong tummy muscles are, if the low back is to work unimpeded.

WHAT ARE THE ACCESSORY MOVEMENTS OF THE SPINE?

Fin-like extensions of bone project from all three sides of the ring at the back of each vertebra. These act as levers on which the small muscles of the back pull. Muscles pass from lever to lever in a variety of directions – vertically, horizontally and diagonally. By the muscle contracting and shortening in length at a given signal, the levers are pulled and released. Depending on the muscle used, each vertebra can be made to move in a variety of directions. It can swivel so that the spine can twist, it can open up at the back so that the spine can bend forwards and vice versa, and it can open up at the side so that the spine can tilt sideways. The amount of movement at any one vertebra is small. It is simply when this movement is magnified, vertebra by vertebra, that we see the generosity of movement our spines can do.

Intersegmental freedom is the vital accessory movement of the spine. In any direction, this is the small gliding movement of shear between one vertebra and the next; each separate vertebra's small movement contributing towards the overall grand movements of the spine. Take, for example, bending forwards. As the spine tips over, there is an incremental forwards slide of the top vertebra on the one underneath. Before the vertebra actually starts to tilt for-wards and a gap opens at the back, the vertebra creeps forward a little on the one below, as we have already seen. This tiny increment of shear adds a profound extra dimension to our overall range of spinal movement. It ensures that the upper vertebra is positioned slightly forwards of the one below before it starts to do its own bit of bend. This is how the spine achieves its phenomenal range of flourishing movement, enabling us to go from touching the toes with the nose on the knees, to fully arching backwards in mid-air . . . well, some people can. If we didn't have shear, if all the vertebrae remained stacked directly over one another as we moved, our movements would be a fraction of what they are. Tight, clipped and jerky.

Considering what a slender machine a spine is, so delicately clothed in rippling efficient musculature, it is amazing what it can do. Look at a child as he stoops to the ground to retrieve a paper dart. In one sweeping arc of movement, he lifts from the ground, unfurling his spine as he goes. He twists sideways as he snakes back through the air and as he passes beyond the vertical, he arches and twists right back, arms held aloft, poised to throw the dart again. Shear, in all that he does, provides the hidden dimension of inter-linking fluidity of movement.

And shear is what we manual therapists are looking for when we feel around in human spines. As you lie prone over a pillow, so that your spine is fully slackened and relaxed, it is surprising how easy it is for us to feel segmental shear. Rather like tinkering up and down a keyboard, the piano keys (the vertebral segments) which are loathe to go are immediately apparent. Manual pressure exerted through our thumbs gives us an instant reading on which are your stiff vertebrae. Actually, it is slightly more complicated than that because any one segment may be free to glide forwards, or to swivel when we push it to the right, but it may be completely blocked when we apply the same sort of manual pressure to the left, for example. Blockage of shear, even if it is isolated to one vertebral level, and even if it is isolated to one component of shear at that level, still constitutes a major flaw in overall spinal movement. To be blunt, it causes havoc. And this sort of simple segmental dysfunction is the ultimate cause of common or garden back pain. It is that simple.

How Does the Low Back Go Wrong?

Generally speaking, two background factors contribute to the demise of the human low back. The first is the long-term impaction of the lower end of the vertebral column, the simple result of our being upright. Like compressing a concertina, it exerts a squashing effect on the fluid-filled discs at the base of the spine. As a result they lose liquid and by the end of the day are significantly flatter. The lower discs lose more fluid than the upper ones and it is only during the night when we lie flat that the discs slowly imbibe fluid and restore themselves to their former stature. The total loss of liquid from all the discs causes us to vary in height by as much two centimetres (nearly an inch) in a day (although it has been found in long-distance runners that the variation can be as much as five centimetres or two inches). As the discs drop down, the vertebral bones settle down closer on to each other. This is not good: the more compressed the spine is, the less it can absorb shock and the more susceptible it is to injury.

The only natural check to this shrinkage is regular injections of full and flamboyant movement. Only this can puff the discs up again. The discs do not have their own blood supply and their only way of replenishing their fluids is by the suction effect induced by movement. Bending over, stretching, arching – any fulsome swinging movement of the whole body will suck fluids in. I don't need to tell you how little of that sort of thing goes on, much worsened, incidentally, by the so-called specialists who command people *never* to touch their toes . . .

The act of sitting makes this much worse. The shrinkage continues on apace. Sitting has its own set of problems, mainly because the pressure within a human disc is greatest when we sit. This causes an even greater net loss of fluid out of the discs at the base of the spine. It would be different if every time we got up from sitting, we bent down to touch our toes. That would be a very good thing. That would prevent the base of the spine impacting further. But as we do so little of that, sitting as a compounder of other factors is a major contributor to back trouble.

The second set of circumstances which discommodes the workings of the human spine is the forwards-bowing of the entire skeleton during everyday activity. If you think about it, we do

30

everything bent. Our position of concentration is always with the frame curled forwards over what we are focusing on. Sitting is bad enough, with the hips kinked up at ninety degrees, but when we add to that the stoop to get the fork to the mouth or the thread through the eye of the needle, the result is a pretty crumpled affair. Even when standing, whether it be making the bed, washing our hands or digging, we are stooping all the time. This disturbs the 'balance of freedom' of the skeleton. You might not be aware of it but the skeleton is developing a lopsidedness of dynamic balance.

Everything goes along well enough as long as you are plain sailing, so to speak. But it is when you hit a force 9 gale that the discrepancies show. This often accounts for your incredulity when you develop back pain after something very trivial. You have a paralysing back problem yet: 'I only sneezed' or 'I was only turning over in bed'. But the problem was brewing, perhaps for all of one's upright life. The spine had been progressively disadvantaged by the compression and the bowing and trouble was waiting in the wings.

In a more specific vein, we should also look at the influence of excessive movement on the intervertebral disc. The discs are the most perishable entity of the spine. More than any other structure, they can be worn out by excessive use. This need not necessarily lead to pain, as you will read in the next section, but it does lead to the deterioration of other parts of the spine. Broadly speaking, as the shock-absorption qualities of the disc diminish, the bony segments of the spine jar together – and they wear out.

Twist or rotation is the weakest movement in the low back. Or put another way, it is the movement which needs the most protection from abuse. The reasons for this are technical but bear relating, not least because of its application in the workplace.

The diagonal mesh of fibres which makes up the wall of the disc helps dampen all movements of the vertebrae. By the wall tautening as the disc opens and goes with the movement, the fibres caution the movement so that the spine doesn't slip off itself. With relative ease it bends forwards and backwards and sideways. It is only the twisting action which causes some concern. This is because of the alternating diagonal alignment of the fibres with each consecutive layer of the disc wall. For any one direction of twist, only the fibres oriented in one direction will steady the movement; all the other fibres will be slackened. They will be flaccid and puckered-up, rather like elastic slackened from its stretch. So you can understand that, as a movement, twist is only half as well controlled. Only half the fibres in the disc wall are restraining the action.

The alignment of bony facets in the lumbar spine do their best to minimise the amount of lumbar twist. The two opposing surfaces are designed to bump up against each other and stop the movement going more than a few degrees. Even so, there is some degree of rotation, and repetitive twisting movements can severely tax a disc wall, especially if lifting is involved as well. This constitutes a combined assault on the disc wall: the increased bulging of the wall as more shock-absorption from the disc is invoked, plus the inherent weakness of twist for the reasons just described. Doing both, lifting and twisting, will eventually lead to trouble. If you add 'bend' as an extra dimension, you are flouting danger even further because bending too makes the walls of a disc bulge. If this is part of shoddy lifting techniques, you have three reasons why the discs wear out. Bending, twisting and lifting all balloon the walls of the discs, the lower ones more than the upper ones. Although the alignment of the facets keeps the twisting movement to a minimum (indeed it is the lumbar spine's most meagre movement), it does take its toll on the facet joints. Wear and tear in this part of the spine is one of the commonest causes of pain in the low back.

The lumbar facet joints also prevent unwanted movement of the spinal segments in another direction, that of forward slippage of one vertebra off the one below. Although the muscles and ligaments enable safe short-term bending of the spine in the manner described above, the ultimate long-term block to the spine slipping off itself is the bony notching of the facets. This can be only too readily demonstrated if the safety mechanism is removed. When for some reason the bony catch is rendered incompetent we see a spine that cannot hold itself together. We see the pathological disorder known as spondylolisthesis – the precarious slip of uppermost vertebra forwards off the lower (usually the fifth lumbar forwards off the sacrum, or the fourth lumbar forwards off the fifth). The incompetence is usually brought about by the bone of the catch breaking so that the lock fails to hold, or it may be a congenital malformation of the bone, or it may be acquired arthritic change as the facet joint is eroded down by wear and tear.

THE COMMON DISORDERS OF THE BACK
Lumbar Spondylosis

This is a fancy name for lumbago or arthritis of the spine. It is really only the ageing process speeded up. The journey can begin early in your life with an accidental 'ricking' of the spine, causing a hiccough in the dancing column of bricks. The result is progressive impaction of its base and the increased bowing of the skeleton. Then out of the blue one fine day, a jarring injury ricks the column during movement.

This sets the process in motion. If there is severe yanking of the tissues during the assault, there will be microscopic bleeding and oozing into the soft-tissue structures which bind the vertebral segment together. The fluid lies around in the tissues and forms the beginnings of scar tissue. As it proliferates, the microscopic scarring invades the delicate machinery of the spine and subtly begins to hamper the free-running ease of the system.

On top of that, you will have an emergency protective spasm by the local muscles locking the segment up tight and stopping it from any further movement. The two factors, the scarring and the muscle spasm, leave the segment more tightly bound in the vertebral chain than it was previously. In other words, if you don't make efforts to get all your original movement back, you will find you have a much stiffer joint. This is serious. It starts the downwards slide in the health of the vertebral segment. Putting it simply: as the movement goes so the health goes.

The disc is the first to suffer because it immediately finds that it cannot plump itself up with fluid. If two vertebral segments are tethered together with soft tissue they are unable to pull apart with normal movement. They then fail to create the suction effect with which the disc drags in fluid (and food) and so the disc silently starves.

By degrees the disc shrinks. It dries out and drops in stature. This has several effects. First, the walls of the disc lose tension. As the pressure within the disc dissipates, the 'squirting' pressure of the nucleus is lost. With the disappearance of the internal disc pressure, the superincumbent weight of the body bears down on the weakened disc walls, causing them to bulge flaccidly under the pressure. This is the picture of the degenerated disc. The disc walls are weak, and are distended further by simple body weight.

The facet joints in the lumbar spine are the next to suffer. With the progressive drying up of the fluid within the discs, each vertebral segment settles down lower on the one below. Like letting air out of a car tyre, this brings the bony surfaces of the facet joints too close together and the surfaces start to grind. The opposing surfaces of cartilage are abraded and the ligamentous capsule containing the facet joint becomes thickened and inflamed. Here in your back, you have a great source of pain.

This is your common or garden backache. The pain can be anywhere in your low back, depending on which structures are the most affected. Pain in the centre indicates that the trouble is probably central impaction of one vertebra ramming down hard on the central body of the one below. Pain at the side, over the dimple of your lower back, over the buttock, or referred down the back of the thigh indicates that the facet joint of that side is suffering.

The pain is a grumbling ache, often made worse by sitting – which impacts it more – and made better by getting up and moving around. You often rub the painful spot and some of you will even pinpoint to the nearest centimetre where the trouble is coming from. Most of your spinal movements will be stiff, and if the problem is one-sided it usually hurts on that side when you bend forwards. It also hurts more to bend away from the side of pain. If the facet joint is suffering an acute flare-up it will be more painful to bend towards the side of pain because it hurts to compress the swollen capsule of the joint. You can often feel a pain down the leg which is referred rather than 'real', the significance of which will become obvious in the section on sciatica on page 37. This is a vague spread of pain, rarely extending beyond the knee, and unaltered by the position of the leg.

If I feel around in your back, I (or any manual therapist) will be able to feel where the problem is. If the pain is central, the vertebral segment will be stiff centrally to shear. Pressure through my thumbs to the central spinous process will feel locally painful, as if the bone itself is bruised, and deep pressure will probably give you a complete re-enactment of your familiar pain.

If the problem is one-sided, it usually means that the central body has swivelled or deviated to one side (the pain usually being to the side where the spinous process has swung), or it may be that the pain is coming from an inflamed facet joint. The facet joint will feel different. Its ligamentous capsule will be enlarged and if the pain is an old problem it will have a tough leathery feel. Whereas the corresponding joint on the other side, if it is healthy, gives an 'empty' bony feel when it is palpated, the problem side feels thick and congested under the skin. When it is pierced deep with the probing pressure of thumbs, it often gives off a characteristic 'sweet' pain. It feels a relief to have the focus of the trouble found.

Like all chronic conditions, this sort of back pain will come and go in bouts but you may suffer sudden even frightening traumatic episodes, punctuating the general monotone of grumblings. This is the acute locking back.

The Acute Locked Back

The degenerative loss of disc height leads to more and more trouble – in particular the settling together of one vertebra down closer on to its neighbour below. When this happens, the ligaments and muscles holding one vertebra snugly on to the other find themselves in a lengthened sloppy state. As the juicy wedge of disc between the two vertebrae shrivels, the slackened soft-tissue binding can no longer prevent incremental movement of the top vertebra on the bottom. The two opposing surfaces of the facet joint slip around in relation to one another and the joint fails in its fundamental task of holding the spine firm at segmental level.

For most of the time, this one sloppy link is lost in the efficient machinery of the rest of the working spine. It is compensated for by its neighbours and is rarely put to the test; its sloppy incompetence is not generally exposed. However, every once in a while the weak link comes to light. Some chance awkward movement will catch it off-guard and down you go like a pack of cards. The loose facet joint will have been caught by a stressful movement and its surfaces will slip askew.

When this happens, the protective muscle spasm is instantaneous. It comes in with a great punching gust which takes your breath away. Your entire body locks up solid and you are usually caught frozen in a half-bend. You can't go up or down. Sometimes you can't get off the floor and you may have to crawl to your bed or the telephone. Many people call straightaway for an ambulance and go off to the hospital but this is not a good idea as hospital staff can do no more for you there than your doctor can do at home with an injection of painkillers and muscle relaxants. Movement is what the segment needs: gentle oscillatory bouncing of the knees to the chest to achieve dis-impaction of the jammed segment and relaxation of the guarding muscles.

These backs can dominate your life: they become the master and you the victim. After such a bout you can carry on well enough for a while, although the back always feels stiff. And then it goes again; usually at the most ridiculous things. As you get worse, you find that your back becomes easier to 'put out' with the bouts becoming more frequent. In between, the resting level of grumbling pain intensifies. As the trouble recurs you will eventually get irritation of the spinal nerve – sciatica.

Sciatica

This is the next phase of the deterioration, pain felt in the leg caused by pinching of the sciatic nerve up in the back. Usually sciatica develops after bouts of pain described above but it is possible to do just one awkward movement and have pain down the leg as a result. But sciatic pain is different from referred pain because it is caused by irritation of the nerve itself. The nerve becames involved in the general inflammation process when it too becomes red and highly irritated.

As the disc loses height and the distension of the disc wall increases, the bulge encroaches closer and closer to the spinal nerve which runs close by. At the same time the capsule of the facet joint encroaches from the other side. With degeneration this capsule has progressively enlarged as well, both from the puckering of the ligamentous binding as the joint settles in closer and also from the actual swelling of the irritated capsular material. The bulging disc walls and the encroaching facet joint lead to inflamed engorgement in the local area. Both conditions can impinge on the delicate spinal nerve in their midst. Inflammation of the nerve is the result.

This gives a particularly nasty sort of leg pain. Often described as shooting red-hot pokers, it can run the whole length of the leg, right down to the toes. Any effort to stretch the nerve, even raising the leg straight off the bed by a few centimetres or a couple of inches, heightens the pain. You may also feel numbness or pins and needles, depending on which fibres in the spinal nerve are being most irritated. If you can stand at all, you stand with the bad leg bent. Your hips may have been thrown out of alignment by the unequal contraction of the muscles on either side of the spine (sciatic scoliosis). The condition takes several weeks to subside since nervous tissue is so unforgiving once it has been irritated. Once again, movement is the therapy.

There has always been much excitement in clinical circles about discs being the sole cause of these troubles. Bulging discs, disintegrating discs, herniating discs, prolapsing discs – all of them have always caused waves of palpable agitation in learned circles. As far as I can see, certainly until recently, the other cause of sciatica – inflamed facet joints – has largely escaped attention. You might say, ignored. Perhaps this accounts for the universal poor showing of laminectomies and discectomies as a surgical method of getting rid of sciatic pain. And I am encouraged even more in my divergent view by a study published recently which showed that 21 per cent of fit healthy symptom-free males in the community – that is, *not* complaining of pain – were found to have herniated lumbar discs on random CT scanning.

The Herniated Lumbar Disc

Sometimes a disc can deteriorate so far that it eventually blows out. When this happens, although there need not be pain, it does further stymie the easy functioning of the spine. It all happens as the walls of the disc get weaker. With degeneration the process just continues on apace, with the internal pressure of the problem disc reducing as the wall gets weaker. With the increasing flaccidity of the disc wall the nucleus can no longer be contained in the centre and it starts to track out radially, through the innermost layers of disc wall. As the body weight bears down the walls get more traumatised, rather like a car tyre running along on its rim. Cracks open up in the wall and it becomes easier for the nucleus to find ways out of the centre of the disc. Eventually, the nuclear material will burst through the last remaining layers of disc wall and spew itself into the cavity of the spinal canal.

This process is not always painful. Disc material alone is not pain-sensitive; it does not have a nerve supply. It is like fingernail and does not mind much whether it is torn or cut or abraded. Only the outer layers of the disc wall are more sensitive and register pain when they are permanently distended by an unresolved disc bulge.

I believe most of any pain felt during these herniation episodes comes from other problems occurring at the same time as the disc is steadily coming closer to rupture. The wider picture may include general inflammation, congestion, as well as the vice-like lock of the muscles. The stealthy trespass and rupture of the nuclear material may occur at any stage while the above picture is evolving. But this topic demands wider discussion and its detail is not within the scope of this book.

What Can You Do About It?

The best thing to do is to keep your spine free from impaction, to avoid the steady degenerative process and also any isolated trauma. Passive elongation of the spine is the fundamental element of accessory movement to try to recapture. If you can achieve this you will have found the most elementary way to reverse the whole of the above process. If you do it early enough in life, it will thwart the progression of the above chain of events. Spinal elongation will even cure a lower back problem already in evidence – even the more sinister ones. Believe it or not, it is *not* actually important what is wrong with your low back – arthritis or disc trouble or worn facet joints. They all benefit from the reversal of the ever-present compression. This simple procedure not only separates your spinal vertebrae but unkinks your entire frame, taking it out of its usual hooped stance and realigning the characteristic 'set' of the skeleton. The best way to achieve spinal separation is to get a BackBlock and do the following exercises. (You can buy a BackBlock by mail order by sending a cheque or money order for £25 [inclusive of postage and packing in the UK – for prices for posting abroad please write to Sunsar Blocks] to Sunsar Blocks, Blenheim Estate Office, Woodstock, Oxfordshire OX20 1PX, UK. All blocks come with comprehensive instructions on how they should be used.)

If you cannot get a BackBlock you can substitute a five-centimetre (two-inch) stack of books. But the advantage of using the BackBlock is that it is designed so you can vary its height easily. You can start off with it at five centimetres (two inches) thick then, as you improve and your spine and your skeleton open out, you can progress to the next height. It is easily portable so you can carry it wherever you go – even in your suitcase.

For maximum benefit, use the BackBlock in the evenings when our spines are most impacted.

EXERCISE 1

The BackBlock

1 Lie on the floor on your back with your knees bent.

2 Lift your bottom off the floor and slide the BackBlock (see page 39) under your bottom. Make sure you don't put it too high up the spine: it should *not* rest under the vertebrae themselves but should go under the sacrum, that hard flat bone at the bottom of the spine.

3 When the BackBlock is in position lower your bottom down on to it and then gradually straighten your legs out along the floor.

are pulling the pelvis off the base of the spine. It should feel agreeably uncomfortable but it may sometimes be difficult to maintain that position for more than a few seconds if the sense of pulling is too great. It should not be agony although it should feel as though it means business; as if it goes straight to the nub of things.

5 After 30 seconds, or more if you can tolerate it, bend your knees again, lift up your bottom and slide the BackBlock out. Lower your bottom on to the floor. It always

4 Relax in this position over the BackBlock. Depending on your degree of 'kink' both at the front of your hips and at your low back, you will feel a pulling sensation in your low back, almost as though your legs

hurts to raise your bottom off the BackBlock. Don't be fazed by this: the longer you have been lying there, the more it will hurt.

6 Always go on to Exercises 2 and 3 after completing this one.

EXERCISE 2

The Knee Bounce

This follows on from Exercise 1.

1 Begin with the BackBlock removed and your knees bent.

2 Grasp one knee with your hands

and bounce it gently on your chest. Do small relaxed bounces and this will calm your back after it has been stretched.

3 Bounce one knee and then the other, for about 30 seconds each.
4 Proceed to Exercise 3.

EXERCISE 3

The Curl Up

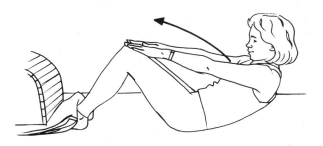

After you use the BackBlock you must always follow with some curl ups. These must be done well; if you do them badly they can actually make your condition worse. You should aim to do up to thirty curl ups daily but it is far better to do eight curl ups well than do thirty hastily and badly.

1 Lie on your back on the floor with your knees bent and your feet secured under a sofa or heavy chair. Do not under any circumstances attempt this with straight legs.

2 Slowly curl your spine up, bringing your nose towards your knees. Do this vertebra by vertebra beginning at the top of your spine until you reach the sitting position. Do not have your hands behind your head because this will encourage you to jerk as you get up which will impact the base of the spine.

3 Gently return to the floor by rolling your hips back and gradually pressing your low back into the floor.

4 Up to thirty curl ups are to be done daily. The longer you spend on the BackBlock the more curl ups you have to do. However, it is not ideal to spend long periods (ten to thirty minutes) on the BackBlock. It is better to break it up into shorter periods of one to two minutes, each time following it with Knee Bounces and the Curl Ups, say eight to ten each time.

EXERCISE 4

The Forwards Bend

As well as opening up the front of the vertebrae you must encourage them to open at the back too. You do this by bending forwards: the exercise that practitioners love to hate.

1 Brace your tummy to reduce the tendency for the dangerous forwards shear. (The strength you gain from doing the curl ups will come in handy here.)

2 Round your lower back and tuck your bottom under. Tip forwards, tightening your tummy and buttocks. If you feel too weak, 'walk' your hands down your legs to begin with.

3 Get low enough to hang – this is where you get some real vertebral separation. Relax and bounce very gently for 15 to 20 seconds.

4 Gradually unfurl yourself upright again. As you get near the vertical position resist the tendency to arch back and flip yourself through the last few degrees. Keep the movement under slow control, with your tummy tightened all the time.

5 Repeat several times all through the day. It is especially useful after lengthy periods of sitting.

EXERCISE 5

The Self-Traction Twist

1 Lie on your back on the floor with your arms out to your sides and your knees bent but touching. Your feet should be flat on the floor, parallel to each other and about thirty centimetres (twelve inches) apart.

2 Keeping your shoulders on the floor, drop your right knee in to the floor so that it rests on the inside of your left ankle. This will cause your right hip to raise off the floor and will create a longitudinal stretch as well as a twist to the base of the spine.

3 Hold that position for 15 seconds

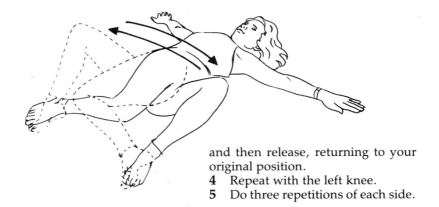

and then release, returning to your original position.

4 Repeat with the left knee.

5 Do three repetitions of each side.

E X E R C I S E 6

The Pelvic Slant

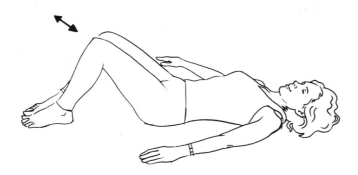

1 Lie on the floor in the same position as for exercise 5.

2 Keeping your feet flat on the floor, push your left knee away from you beyond the other knee. This will cause your pelvis to tilt sideways. The knee will not go very far forwards, only about four centimetres (less than two inches) beyond the right knee.

3 Hold that position for 10 seconds then release.

4 Repeat with the other side.

5 Repeat six times, alternating sides.

EXERCISE 7

The Sciatic Stretch

You will need a belt or strap for this.

1 Lie on your back on the floor and by bending the left knee, hook a belt or strap around the sole of your left foot.

2 With your left arm out beside you on the floor to act as a counter-balance, hold the strap in your right hand.

3 Keeping your left leg straight, pull the foot up towards your right armpit.

4 Let it continue on and fall over the floor out to the right.

5 Hold that position for 60 seconds, keeping the tension of the left leg by pulling on the strap.

6 Release and do the same with the other leg.

7 Repeat three times for each leg.

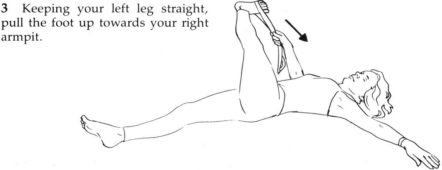

EXERCISE 8

The Ultimate Backwards Arch

This is only for the advanced exerciser.

1 Lie on your back on the floor with your knees bent and your feet flat on the floor. Bring your hands above your head and back on the floor under your shoulders, fingers pointing down your back.

2 Lift your bottom off the floor then, pushing through your arms, take your weight through the top of your head.

3 As a final thrust, straighten your arms and push yourself up into a backwards arch. Hold for 15 seconds then relax.

Chapter Six

THE THORACIC SPINE

WHAT IS THE THORACIC SPINE?

The thoracic spine is the middle part of the back. It goes from the base of the neck, just below the prominent bump, down to high waist level where the lumbar spine starts. The thoracic spine takes on the most visible 'look' of our posture; the ramrod back of the sergeant major or the round shoulders of the slouch. From the side view, its natural curve gives us our gently protruding back so that as a whole the spine exhibits a gentle 'S' bend from top to bottom. At the base is the hollow for the low back, above that the gentle hump of the thorax, and then another scoop for the neck.

The twelve thoracic vertebrae are smaller and more delicate than the lumbar ones, and their side projections (transverse processes) are longer and finer as well. The tails of the vertebrae, the spinous processes, are long and instead of pointing back horizontally, as they do in the neck and the lumbar region, they droop downwards rather like fish scales. Twelve pairs of ribs are attached to the sides of the thoracic vertebrae, and each rib actually straddles the junction between one vertebrae and the next. This somewhat impedes the mobility of this part of the spine. To add further clutter to the tethering of the ribs to the spine, there is another connection on either side, between the rib and the tip of the transverse processes. This is only a glancing articulation, as the rib sweeps past the vertebra on its way round the chest wall.

The first ribs start much higher than you would think; about the level of a necklace if worn at the base of the neck. You can feel them by digging deeply with your fingers into the muscle bulk at either side of the base of your neck. All the ribs come forwards from either side of the spine at the back and curve around the side of the chest to meet up either side of the breastbone (the sternum) at the front.

The ribs make the chest into a semi-collapsible cage whose volume is altered by muscle action. When you breathe in, your

Side view of thoracic spine showing the hemi-cage of the ribs.

Back

Breast bone or sternum

Front

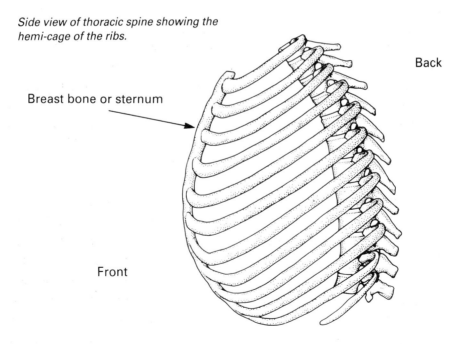

diaphragm contracts along with the other muscles of respiration and so the diameter and therefore the volume of your chest cage is increased. This automatically lowers the pressure within the chest so that air flows in. (It is a myth that we wilfully suck in breaths.) After a breathable volume of air has gone in, we pause for a second or two and then breathe out. The out-breath happens when the muscles relax. The elastic recoil of the rib cage lets the chest cavity return to its former volume and we expel a quantity of air. You can see that the capacity of the lungs is therefore directly related to the elasticity of the soft tissues and the hinges (joints) of the chest.

HOW DOES THE THORACIC SPINE WORK?

This is the least mobile part of the human spine. Both the presence of the ribs and the shape of the spinous processes of the thoracic spine hamper mobility. The least mobile movements are backwards and sideways bending. The most mobile is rotation or twist. The movement of the ribs during respiration is rather like bucket handles; up and out as we breathe in, and down and in again as we breathe out. Whatever the thoracic spine does in the way of every-day movement, the 'respiring' ribs have to come along too. This is quite a feat of co-ordination when you consider the life-sustaining endeavours of the elastic chest cage, relentlessly sucking in and expelling air, while at the same time the thoracic spine and the ribs are accommodating all those other less essential tasks – like shrugging your shoulders to music, or twisting to reverse the car, or running up to throw a javelin.

Apart from its role in supporting the cage of the thorax, the thoracic spine's chief function is to provide background mobility for the free-swinging antics of the head and neck. Although the neck itself is very mobile, it relies a great deal on the mobile-base properties of the thoracic spine. By positioning itself under the neck and going some way towards the overall movement of the neck, this part of the spine sets the stage for movement above. As described in the previous chapter on low backs, generosity of movement is made possible because, as one travels further up the spine, the centre of gravity of each vertebra is placed just a little bit further on into the movement than its neighbour below. This means that by the time you get up to the top of the column – to the eyes or the ears or the mouth – you have phenomenal generosity of mobility, mainly because of the freedom offered by the thorax. If you didn't have this deep-seated thoracic contribution, you would find that your neck not only had a fraction of its full range of movement but there would also be insupportable wear and tear where your neck emerged from your shoulders.

WHAT ARE THE ACCESSORY MOVEMENTS OF THE THORACIC SPINE?

Like all parts of the spine, the important accessory movements are the glide, slip and shuffle between one vertebral segment and the next. Each vertebra should possess its own freedom in all these directions – as well as its individual ability to swivel. In the thorax, swivel is the most important element because of the ribs.

You could describe the ribs as being lashed on to the sides of the spine. All the way up and down they are tethered to the sides of the vertebrae by a criss-cross of ligaments. Rotation is the only movement which keeps the vertebrae free from the smothering clutches of that ligamentous bind. Important as it is that the ribs hold on, they quickly cause problems if they hold on too tight. Not only will a tight rib-to-spine (costo-vertebral) joint restrict the rib's own ability so that it cannot move up and out as it should to open the chest and suck in air, but it will also tether the vertebra itself and festoon it with debility. A tight costo-vertebral junction will always mean a tight rib and a stiff vertebra.

Experienced hands can always feel the mobility of ribs and vertebrae. We do it by lying you down prone over a pillow with your arms relaxed beside you. By cruising around along your spine with our thumbs, we can immediately feel where the trouble is. The problem vertebrae will usually be slightly recessed but often they may actually be more prominent. More importantly, they will feel stiff to easing pressure from one or several directions. What is also interesting is that when testing for rotatory freedom in the thoracic spine is that the problem vertebrae will always be freer to rotate one way than the other. I suspect this relates to the mechanics of the original mechanical 'glitch' which caused the problem in the dim dark past. The tail of the vertebra, the spinous process, is swung off to one side as if the vertebra has become cast or frozen in the position it was when it sustained its injury.

I had a patient the other day who complained of severe pain in his abdomen, high up under the lower end of his breastbone. Since all his abdominal tests had come up with nothing he came to me. He was unable to sleep at night and was rapidly going downhill. Sure enough, on palpation of his upper thoracic spine, he had several vertebrae between his shoulder blades which were prominent and thickened and, when pressured with my thumbs, reproduced his familiar pain. More importantly, these three vertebrae were all rotated to the right. When I asked about the details of the incident which brought the trouble on, he related that he had reversed his car into a pole while looking backwards over his left shoulder. (Don't ask me about his eyesight.) Now, some several months later, these three vertebrae still hold the position of the original injury. His vertebrae remain swung to the right and the accessory movement this man lacks is rotation of the vertebrae to the left. (When you twist the body left the spines of the vertebrae swing right.)

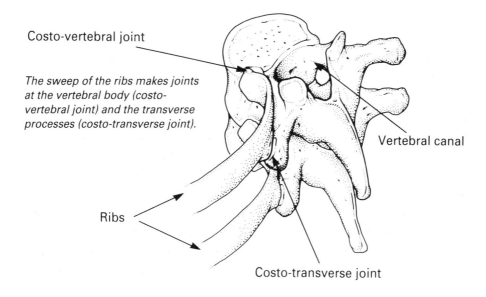

Costo-vertebral joint

The sweep of the ribs makes joints at the vertebral body (costo-vertebral joint) and the transverse processes (costo-transverse joint).

Vertebral canal

Ribs

Costo-transverse joint

Anomalies of accessory movement of the vertebrae are not all we can feel: just as interesting is the rib itself. We can feel the rib in two places: where it makes its passing union with the tip of the transverse process of the vertebra (the costo-transverse junction), and also out at the rib angle, where the rib changes direction and goes around the chest wall. You can feel it like a steel band around a barrel. Unlike healthy ribs which yield obligingly to pressure, problem ribs sit up and rebuff pressure and this is usually painful. Closer in to the spine, over the costo-transverse junction, the joint itself feels thickened and leathery and unilateral spin of this side of the vertebra is sluggish.

How Does the Thoracic Spine Go Wrong?

Apart from the accessory freedom just described, the chest itself is rather set upon by the muscles of the upper arm and shoulder blade. In the case of the arm, the muscles bind themselves in an almost cloying fashion across the upper end of the chest cage, fanning themselves across the outside of the wall. From here, their fibres funnel in to attach on to the head of the humerus, the upper bone of the arm. For this reason strenuous work with the arms tends to make the upper part of the chest muscle-bound; the stronger the arm, particularly the upper arm, the tighter the chest. Depending on the predominance of the muscle groups being used, the curve of the spine can also be influenced. Without simplifying the matter too much, powerful shoulder-blade work often leads to a too-straight spine, whereas powerful arm work often leads to roundness of the upper back. Arm work, although it can contribute to postural changes, is rarely a cause of pain in its own right – unless you are a mad-keen sportsman.

Ultimately, if one teams the naturally occurring tightness of the chest with acquired changes to the spinal curve as a result of over-zealous arm or shoulder work, and superimposes these on congenital disturbances of alignment of the spine – you have a real recipe for trouble. Congenital kinks and bends of the spine make by far the greatest contribution towards grumbling pains over the back of the chest wall. The spines that give the most trouble are those with an 'S' bend when viewed from the side (scoliosis), or those which exhibit too great or too flat an arch when viewed from the side.

THE COMMON DISORDERS OF THE THORACIC SPINE
Thoracic Kyphosis

This is an increase in the rounding of the back in the thoracic area. It is usually associated with drooping of the shoulders and the head being carried too far forwards in front of the line of the body. It can be an inherited congenital condition or it may be acquired by lazy habits of posture as well as poorly-balanced powerful work with the arms. The pain resulting from this condition is usually slow to come on. You may have known of the anomaly of your posture for years but only recently been bothered by any pain. The usual site is across the top of your shoulders where you will have a tired gnawing pain at the angle of your neck. The pain will usually be worse on the side of your dominant hand and will be heightened by tension and also by carrying anything heavy.

The greatest problem is created by carrying your head too far forwards in front of the line of gravity, simply because the head is so heavy. The trapezeii muscles, which run down either side of the neck from the base of the skull and fan out across the shoulders and down the back, have the job of bracing the shoulder blades and keeping the head back, retracted in line with the shoulders. When the head falls forwards they are forced to act like horse's reins, trying to pull the head back over the support of the rest of the spine. But because the head is such a weight and because so many activities, especially precision ones, involve bending the head down, the order is a tall one. The constant postural strain causes the muscles to develop a low-grade persistent spasm: that twinging pain which makes you want to pummel, bash and even pinch the muscles to get some relief. The long-term spasm of the trapezeii also creates further immobility of the chest. The tension on the 'reins' keeps the vertebrae of the neck and thorax permanently bunched up so that the section of spine underlying the muscles compresses and eventually loses mobility.

Powerful arm work can make a kyphosis worse. It may compress the mobility of the chest and cause the shoulders to stay permanently hunched forward. The chest itself may even appear sunken. The pectoral muscles, in particular, are responsible for this. They take origin in a fan-shaped spread across the front of each side of the upper chest wall. If they are particularly powerful or tight, they will not only hamper the ability of the ribs to open and the chest to expand but they will also pinch the shoulders forwards and accentuate the poking forwards of the neck.

There are a couple of top international tennis players I could name who suffer from this problem. Perhaps a predominance of service and forehand strokes in their game, at the expense of the opening-out backhand shots, means that the pectorals tighten and shorten with overuse. Good as these players might be, they would just be that much better if they balanced up their strokes a bit. Their skeleton would be better balanced and so would their game and they would not be storing up a heap of trouble for themselves in the form of tennis elbow and problems of strains of the shoulder and upper back. (These are covered later in the book.)

As you will see in the exercise section on pages 55–60, many of the stretches for the rounded upper back pay particular attention to opening the shoulders.

Sergeant Major's Back

Problems which arise from the thoracic spine being too straight are of an altogether different nature: all to do with the difficulty of the ribs keying into the spine. If, through the spine being too straight, the ribs fail to approach from the angle which suits their anatomical alignment, the junction made will be a difficult one. As a result all movements of this part of the spine – not only breathing but everyday functional movement as well – carry with them a rather laboured action of the ribs themselves. Breathing becomes hampered and of necessity shallower. (Easy to see, incidentally, why it is so important to get the posture of asthmatic children right.) In short, there will be subtle strain at the rib-to-spine junctions – the costo-vertebral joints. You can see this strain with thoracic spines which are too round as well although in these cases the usual feature is discomfort across the shoulders and the base of the neck.

Poor functioning of the costo-vertebral joints causes a variety of aches and pains all over the chest wall. They can be felt above or below the shoulder blade; they can be felt in a girdle distribution following the line of a rib; they can be felt in the front of the chest like a knife coming through the chest; they can even be felt like a 'stitch' in the side (and in my time, I've seen many a gall bladder removed in search of the source of this very pain).

There is another more obscure manifestation of this rib trouble and that is the 'dead arm' syndrome. If you have this problem, you complain that one of your arms doesn't feel part of you. There is a diffuse pain throughout your arm and often your hand feels achey so that you want to squeeze it and nurse it with your other hand. But there are other things that you complain of too; other more mystifying feelings. Your arm often feels cold or hot. Sometimes your fingers feel stiff or the veins on the back of your hand stand up, especially if your hand is painful. You often want to position your arm over your head if you are lying on your back in bed, because this is how the arm feels most comfortable.

In these cases, it is thought that the too-straight spinal alignment disturbs the natural autonomic function of the arm. The autonomic nerve system regulates the activities which happen automatically without your consciously controlling them: things like the diameter of the blood vessels of the arm, the facility of sweating, and the goose-flesh phenomenon as well. The nervous lacework of this system drapes itself in a chain up and down either side of the spine, just superficial to (nearer the surface) the costo-vertebral junctions. It is thought that irregularities in the function of these junctions causes irregularity in function of the autonomic nervous system with the result that you feel pain in your arm along with the other symptoms already described.

53

Scoliosis

This is lateral twist of the spine into one or two concave hoops so that when viewed from behind the spine exhibits an 'S' shaped twist. Scoliosis is usually a condition that you are born with but it can also be acquired if one leg is shorter than the other. The problems with scoliosis lie in the same factors outlined above: those of disturbances of spinal alignment and those of fitting the ribs into the spine.

Scoliosis looks as if the spine has been frozen as a wobble passed through it. There is a static twisting and buckling of the column throughout its length. This causes the stacked vertebrae to slew round on one another, pinching together at the front and sides of the vertebrae as the spine bends in and out of twisted hoops. Drastic as this may sound, scoliosis need not be severe. Mild scoliosis is an extremely common condition; so common in fact that radiologists often fail to comment upon it in their X-ray reports. However, even in its most mild form, it can be a ready source of pain.

There are several parts of the scoliotic spine which cause pain. Firstly, the vertebrae at the apex of each curve suffer wear and tear by being pinched where the hoop changes direction; the inside of the curve rather than the out. Secondly, pain results at other levels of the spine where there is the most twist of the vertebrae. This is created by the shearing strain of the stacked vertebrae slipping sideways in the 'leaning' sections of spine. Lastly, most of the pain comes from the rib junctions as the working ribs attempt to key themselves into the sides of a bucking and rolling spine.

The pain is a conglomeration of those described in kyphotic and too-straight spines but the distribution is more extensive. In fact this is a feature of scoliotic spines; the pain is everywhere. Children are often dismissed as malingerers when they describe a pain that criss-crosses left and right, up and down from the base of the spine to the skull. These, along with headaches and pains in the legs, usually turn out to be accurate descriptions of just this condition.

WHAT CAN YOU DO ABOUT IT?

In rectifying these common problems of the upper back, we must set about rectifying the abnormalities of spinal alignment. Easier said than done, of course. All the conditions described above have been acquired over time and it is not a simple matter to undo them with the wave of a wand. But even the remotest degree of loosening of all the structures named above will bring quite astonishing relief. Quite quickly you will sense a greater freedom of movement and notice the pain fading. Even if pain is not an issue for you and you simply do not like the look of your back or the way you stand, the same exercise will bring benefits. If the back is too rounded, we must get it to go straighter. If the back is too straight, we must introduce some bend, and if it is twisted, we must work towards getting it unbent.

EXERCISE 1

The Right Angle

This is good for those with a round-shouldered back. It looks simple but is extremely taxing.

1 Find a clear space of wall with some uncluttered floor in front of it. Sit sideways into the wall with your bottom as near to the wall as you can get it.

2 Roll on to your back and swing your legs up against the wall. Stretch your arms out along the floor above your head. You should find yourself in a right-angled bend at the hips.

3 Do not allow your knees to bend or your bottom to lift off the floor. Hold this position for 2 to 5 minutes.

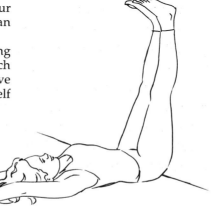

4 You can make this exercise more taxing by interlacing your fingers and turning them palm-up above your head – without bending your elbows.

5 To release from the exercise, bend your legs on the wall, and round your back. With your knees bent, tip on to your side on the floor. NB The longer you have been in this position, the more cast you feel on release. Make small wriggling movements on your side to soften your spine before getting up.

EXERCISE 2

The Thoracic Arms Tangle

You will need a kitchen chair for this. This is good for the scoliotic back as well as the too-straight upper back.

1 Sit towards the front of a chair with your feet on the floor and your spine held straight.

2 Take both arms out in front of you with the upper arms held parallel to the floor and both elbows bent to a ninety-degree angle.

3 Lift your right arm over your left at the elbows so that the outer aspect of the arms touch each other.

4 Twine your forearms around each other so both palms are in apposition to each other (albeit with the left palm lower down the forearm). Keep your upper arms held up parallel to the floor.

5 Now raise the whole tangled arm complex up as high in front of your face as possible. Hold for 15 seconds then relax. You will feel a pulling sensation in your ribs where they attach to the spine in the upper back. The higher you go the more they will pull.

6 Repeat three times then reverse the position of the arms and repeat another four times.

EXERCISE 3

The Thoracic Side Bend

You will need a kitchen chair for this.

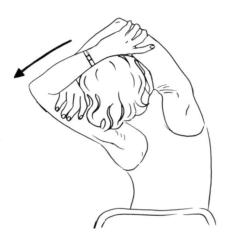

1 Sit towards the front of a chair with your feet on the floor and your spine held straight.
2 Bend each arm to ninety degrees and hold each elbow with your other hand.
3 Raise both your arms above your head and pull them right back so your upper arms are as far behind your ears as possible.
4 In this position bend your trunk sideways to the left making sure you keep your arms held high and back. Hold the position for 15 seconds, breathing normally all the time, then release.
5 Repeat three more times to the left then change sides and do this four times to the right.

EXERCISE 4

The Twist On All Fours

This is good for the scoliotic back.
1 Start on your hands and knees on the floor.
2 Turn your right hand palm-up with the fingers pointing diagonally back between your left hand and your left knee.
3 Slide this right hand between your left hand and knee and as far out the other side as it is possible to go. As you do this let your right shoulder twist under and the top of your head and the tip of your right shoulder touch the floor. You will need to bend your left elbow to allow maximum movement to take place.
4 Hold the position for 15 seconds before returning to your original hands and knees position.
5 Repeat three more times to the left and then change sides and do this four times to the right.

EXERCISE 5

The Floor Twist

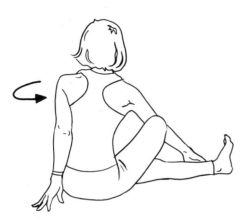

1 Sit on the floor with both legs stretched out in front of you.
2 Place your right leg over the left knee and allow your right foot to rest on the floor on the outside of your left knee.
3 Turning your trunk to the left, push your right elbow against the inside of your right knee which levers you further to the left.
4 Hold the position for 30 seconds and then release and relax before repeating twice.
5 Repeat three times in the opposite direction.

EXERCISE 6

The Plough

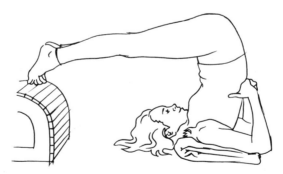

This is good for people with a too-straight back. By bearing weight on the shoulders and the upper ribs this exercise gently forces the thoracic spine into a hoop, with a splaying-out effect of the 'fish scales' of the thoracic vertebrae. You will need a robust pillow and a small stool.

1 Position the stool about forty-five centimetres (eighteen inches) away from the pillow on the floor.
2 Lie on your back on the floor with the pillow positioned crossways under your shoulders and your head free on the floor.

3 Raise both legs up and swing them up and over your head so that your feet rest on the stool behind your head. Make this movement smooth not jerky. Support your bottom with your hands (arms bent at the elbow) and hold this position for as long as you can – up to 5 minutes if possible – relaxed and breathing evenly all the time. The pillow should be positioned to allow a step-down at the point where the thorax becomes the neck and this spares the neck from too much pushing under. The more uncomfortable the neck feels, the higher the pillow step-down should be. You will find the exercise hard to do at first; a pull on the neck and hard to breathe, but even holding it for 15 seconds helps. You will feel a mixed sensation of stretch and pain in your middle back which will be relieved only by relaxing into the pain and gently breathing through it.

4 As you practise this you will find that you can progress the movement further by removing the stool and allowing your knees to bend down on to your forehead. Because your head is lower than your heart and because your shoulder girdle is being moved away from the head, this is one of the most relaxing positions for meditation.

EXERCISE 7

The BackBlock

This is good for the round-shouldered back.

1 Position the BackBlock (see page 39) on its flattest side lengthwise on the floor under your back at the apex of your roundness.

2 Lie back over the BackBlock and allow your head to loll back on the floor and your hands to relax at your side.

3 Maintain this position for about 2 minutes then gently roll off the side of the BackBlock.

4 After practice you will be able to progress this exercise by stretching your arms along the floor above your head, keeping the elbows straight and clasping your fingers and turning your palms upwards. You can also progress it by putting the BackBlock on its middle height.

EXERCISE 8

The Tennis Ball Release

* (not graded according to difficulty) A faulty rib junction behaves exactly like a rusty hinge and so will respond beautifully if you apply direct pressure to the hinge itself. You will need a new tennis ball for this exercise.

1 Lie on your back on the floor with your knees bent and feet flat on the ground.

2 Raise yourself up slightly and manoeuvre the ball under yourself so that it sits exactly under the painful spot near the spine.

3 Lower some of your weight down on to the ball and wriggle around on it so that it agitates the rusty rib function as you roll back and forth over it. Make the movements of the ball small so that you spend most of the time with the ball exactly under that painful spot. There will be a sweet pain: agony but ecstasy.

4 Continue for as long as you can bear it but for no more than 3 minutes to avoid bruising.

Chapter Seven

THE NECK

WHAT IS THE NECK?

The neck is that fine slender structure atop the shoulders which swivels the head. It is an exquisite though vulnerable piece of machinery. How could it not be, harbouring such elaborate freedom to nod and shake and tilt sideways, while at all times carrying that fearfully heavy head? But the neck is not merely a mobile tube with the head sitting on top; it is more than just a dancing support structure. Neuro-physiologically it is alive with nerve pathways, almost like an extension of the brain. A dense lacework of nervous hook-ups drapes itself all over the neck's bony, jointed column, threading in and around the free-swinging vertebrae, not to mention around the joints between each vertebra. This neural matter has many functions. For example, some participate in the more primitive functions of the central nervous system such as monitoring balance. Others control the blood supply to the brain, others supply power to the muscles of the arms and sensation to the skin. In all, a dauntingly sophisticated variety.

The neck consists of seven vertebrae from the base of the skull to the top of the back. Each vertebra is made up of a roundish central

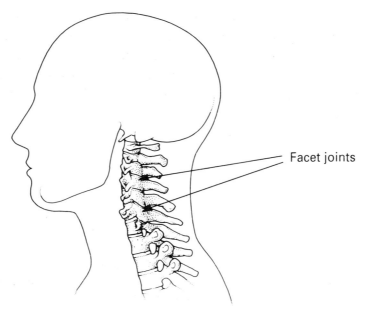

The side view of the neck. The neck starts right up in the skull.

body and two wing-like projections out either side and a fin-like one out the back. Each vertebra articulates above and below with its neighbours where these side projections lie on top of one another – making the apophyseal or facet joints. The intervertebral discs sit between each vertebra, just like all the other vertebral levels in the thorax and low back, as seen in chapters 5 and 6. But there is one significant difference in the neck vertebra-disc-vertebra joints. The vertebral bodies actually pinch together and meet at the sides, making a joint bone-to-bone beyond the disc. These are called the joints of Luschka and their presence is significant: as the discs are contained, disc prolapses and herniations in the neck are rare.

The top two vertebrae are unusual since they alone make marked contributions to neck mobility. The first vertebra is called the atlas and it connects directly with the base of the skull. Two rounded bumps or condyles on the bottom of the skull, rather like the rockers of a rocking chair, fit exactly into two scooped-out hollows in the first vertebra below. This allows a nodding action of the head and it provides about twenty degrees of overall neck flexion. The second vertebra (called the axis) is largely made up of one central long projection or peg which sticks up through a round central hole in the first vertebra, like poking your index finger up through a circle made from your other index finger and thumb. This allows the head and the first vertebra to swivel on the second vertebra and it gives the neck an extra dimension of twisting ability.

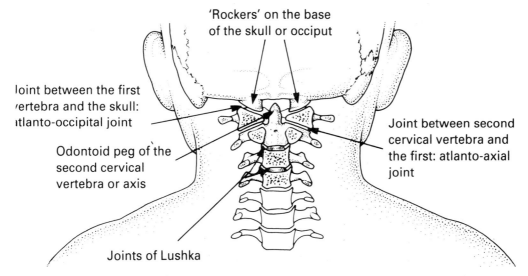

'Rockers' on the base of the skull or occiput

Joint between the first vertebra and the skull: atlanto-occipital joint

Odontoid peg of the second cervical vertebra or axis

Joint between second cervical vertebra and the first: atlanto-axial joint

Joints of Lushka

Nodding happens at the atlanto-occipital joint (skull and first cervical vertebra) and swivel at the atlanto-axial joint (cervical 1 and 2).

How Does the Neck Work?

It is the exquisite combinations of movement which give the neck its generous and competent freedom. Really, its range of movement is extraordinary; 180 degrees of rotation and almost as much in the nodding up and down movement, not to mention all the other possible combinations of these two. As discussed in the last chapter on the thorax, the spine below the neck provides the background mobility for the neck and the neck spans the breach between the shoulders and the skull like a delicate suspension bridge. The neck is clothed front and back with muscles, like stays which anchor a flag-pole. During a contraction of the ones at the front say (the flexors), they shorten and draw the neck over, bending the head and neck down. The muscles down the back of the neck, called the extensors or para-spinal muscles, work to hold the neck upright against gravity and also to arch the neck backwards. The rotatory

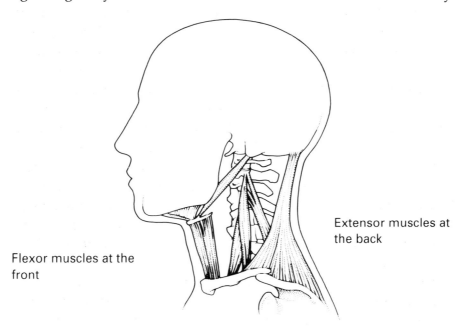

Flexor muscles at the front

Extensor muscles at the back

The angle of pull of most of the neck muscles is very nearly straight.

movement of the neck is provided by the two sternomastoid muscles, the two prominent strands of muscle at the front of the neck and by the smaller muscles which pass from vertebra to vertebra in a diagonal direction.

The facet joints have a very significant role to play in checking all movements of the neck, particularly in controlling the exuberance of twist. They are the buffers or doorstops which prevent one vertebra rotating too far and dislocating off the one below.

WHAT ARE THE ACCESSORY MOVEMENTS OF THE NECK?

Like the rest of the spine, the accessory movements of this part of the spine are the incremental gliding and shuffling movements between one vertebra and the next. However in the neck, because of its lavish freedom, there is an added emphasis on the mobility of the facet joints. Their freedom is the vital accessory movement of the neck. As described above, they act as the bony blocks to brake the movement between one vertebra on the next. Having said that, they do allow a lot of freedom. Remarkable freedom. The adjacent surfaces of each facet joint are not propped up in vertical opposition to one another, they are sloped. This means that as the top vertebra swivels on the bottom one, say, it has to slide up the sloping hill of the surface of the bone below, the steepness of the hill and the increasing tension of the capsule of the facet joint providing the vital impediment to the movement going too far. In the neck, there is much more movement in this regard than elsewhere in the spine. The critical balance is providing as much facet joint slide as possible to give the neck full rotation (and other movements) without letting it attenuate too far, resulting in the top bone surface going over the edge. The critical balance is between too much and too little accessory movement.

You can imagine the discord that would be set up if one set of facet joints at one level of the spine starts sticking. Equally, you can imagine how wonky the general harmony of the neck will be, if a facet joint on one side is jammed while its partner on the other side is free-running: one facet joint in the chain not gliding and shuffling properly, when all the others do. And you can imagine the discord if there is a random scatter of facet joints all over the place which are too claggy and gummed-up for easy movement.

It is possible to feel accessory freedom of facet joints, particularly of the neck. They are like a chain of knobs down either side of the neck, in the back part of the side of your neck, just in front of the thick cable of muscle running up both sides of the neck. People often think of them as 'nodules', especially if they are swollen and inflamed and sore, but they are not nodules, they are joints. Feeling them with our thumbs, evaluating them for how they feel, how well they glide and if there is loss of accessory movement, is how people like me spend a large part of our working day. Although they are not the only things which can go wrong, it is the facet joints which give us the most accurate reading on neck function.

How Does the Neck Go Wrong?

The usual problem with necks is a too-stiff thorax. Denied the full benefit of full background mobility from here, the neck readily gets itself into trouble. Then, it seems, all the natural features of the neck seem to work against it – the unwieldiness of the neck and the heaviness of the head, not to mention the latent imbalance of the muscle hold at the front and back of the neck. When you recall how jaunty the neck is and how it joggles along on the top of the shoulders as we move, it is not surprising how easy it is to overtax the guarding qualities of the facet joints.

Of course, the ligaments of the spine do an admirable job of binding the vertebral stack of bricks together. And the muscles also play an invaluable part in stability. Even so, the buck stops at the bony block of one facet on another. In the following section I will describe how the wear and tear of this braking mechanism takes its toll on these facet joints. You will see how, as a routine happening, the facet joints are assaulted, simply in their role in cautioning flamboyant neck mobility and how other more sinister complications can follow on from this. But meanwhile, here are some other 'normal' features which add to the general strain on a neck.

The angle of pull of the muscles in the neck can subtly fuel trouble, especially if the neck has gone past the point where it has hurt itself. Both the muscles at the front and the back of the neck have an extremely poor angle of pull. Some of them lie in a completely straight line so that when they contract and bend the neck forwards, for example, they simply pinch the front of the vertebrae together. Their action involves a lot of simple compression to bring about the overall movement they require. The same is true of the extensors, the muscles at the back of the neck, although they are slightly more efficient. Even so their action also compresses the neck, bunching it together like a concertina, all because their angle of pull is so bad.

For comparison's sake, the muscles of the calf which attach to the back of the heel, have an extremely advantageous angle of pull. By shortening in a contraction, they pull the back of the heel up which tips the front of the foot down. It is very fortunate that the action is made so easy, since this muscle group has one of the most arduous tasks of the body – lifting our weight and propelling us forwards in the act of walking. The energy expended by the calf muscle is put to full use in bringing about the required movement at the ankle.

Not so with the neck, where part of the action of, say, the flexors at the front of the neck is wasted on the unwanted element of compressing the neck together. This is not such a problem when we are upright when the simple weight of the head if anything helps to nod and roll the head about. But it is a much greater problem if we are horizontal. It is quite difficult to get your head up off the floor. It is a murderous angle of pull, especially without a pillow. This explains why getting up in the morning, that first action of the day in getting your head off the pillow, can be so taxing.

The main point about the compression resulting from the muscles' line of pull is that their action can annoy the neck if its function is already below par. It doesn't even matter much what is causing the problem in the neck – a disc to vertebra junction or facet joint junction. Any dysfunction of the spine will be made worse by compression; the longitudinal clamping of the neck, jamming the segments together and aggravating them further.

Clenching of the muscles at the front of the neck is more a feature of acute conditions of the neck, whereas spasm of the muscles at the back of the neck plays more of a role with chronic disorders of the neck. This relates to the differing nature of the two sets of muscles. As discussed in the chapters on shoulders and, to a lesser degree, on wrists, we see that there are postural muscles and phasic muscles. The muscles of the back of the neck are postural because their function is to keep the head up on top of the shoulders. This means they are working constantly against gravity, and so have to maintain a perpetual degree of low-intensity contraction for as long as we stay upright. If the neck is bad, there will also be an element of protective muscle spasm added to this postural tone and this is what leads to the classical symptoms of 'tension' in the neck. The continuing effect of this compression on the facet joints is not a good one. Under the pressure of the vice-like hold of the muscles, the joint capsules start to bloat and distend and their easygoing action becomes more and more hampered. As the joint remains held it becomes further inflamed which leads on to other complications, most notably irritation of the spinal nerve.

So in summary: the mobility of the thoracic spine, the heaviness of the head, the angle of pull of the neck muscles, the potential for puffiness of the facet joint capsule, and the proximity of a generously free-wheeling bony column to a highly sensitive nervous network can easily get our necks into trouble.

THE COMMON DISORDERS OF THE NECK
An Acute Neck

This is usually the result of a jolt to the neck; some chance awkward movement which strained the neck and 'ricked' one of the joints. It can be something dramatic like taking a swing at a golf ball that doesn't connect, or turning to look behind you as you go down a step. It may even be the unwelcome event of a whiplash injury from a car accident. Or on the other hand, it can be something much more subtle, like sleeping awkwardly on a pillow or simply undergoing a stressful emotional period.

It is usually some fluke, unexpected movement which catches the stabilising mechanisms unawares. This sneaks under the protective vigilance of the postural mechanism and, before the muscles can react in time to control or prevent the movement, the congruent surfaces of the facet joint slip slightly askew and then are jammed too far over on one another. The joint is strained by the excessive movement and the ligaments holding the two surfaces are tugged. The usual process of inflammation ensues: microscopic tearing of the fibres of the ligaments and the joint capsule; and effusion of fluid and if severe enough, blood. This oozes into the tissues around the joint and unless there is plenty of movement early on, the swelling stays there and solidifies into the beginnings of scar tissue. The surrounding muscles then go into protective muscle spasm to splint the joint and protect it from further hurting itself. Because of the reasons outlined above, the muscle hold rapidly makes things worse.

These are described as 'acute' necks. If you have one you will typically be guarded in all your neck movements and you will tend to carry your head cocked to one side, to be in the most comfortable position. But it is sudden movements which cause you the most worry. Any jerk of the neck will cause an agonising stab of pain up through your neck into your head and sometimes down into your shoulder as well. All movements are restricted, although if you take your time and do them slowly, you will find there is always more movement there than you think. Getting up in the morning is one of the most agonising things that you can do in the whole day. You find you cannot lift your head off the pillow and you may even have to lever your hands in behind your head to lift it up, or pull your head up by the hair. The trapezius muscle at the side, the one that webs up the side of your neck, has a much more efficient angle of pull. Therefore, it often hurts less to turn yourself on your side and lift yourself sideways off the pillow, a trick that you probably do without even realising it.

You can get a similar type of pain if you are sitting in a car and the car acclerates. The co-contraction of the neck muscles clenches the neck together as it tries to keep the neck still. It compresses the neck, further inflamming the swollen joint, and greatly adds to the resting level of discomfort.

This is the short-term picture of a simple acute episode. Reasonably quickly the muscle guarding will fade and normal movement will resume except, invariably, you do not quite get back your full complement of movement. That one facet joint will never again come up with as much movement as the others in the chain, and it will go on to fuel the chronic neck condition described later as cervical spondylosis.

Brachial Neuralgia

It is possible that the acute episode does not subside with time and that the injured joint goes on to become more locked, more engorged and more inflamed. The small joint remains caught in the gnawing clench of muscle spasm so that the normal cleansing access and egress of blood through the joint is compressed to a sluggish trickle. The joint becomes more and more inflamed: angry, bloated and locked out of movement by its very own distension. The inflammation spreads to the neighbouring tissues and then the close proximity of the spinal nerve causes serious complications.

Nervous tissue is extremely sensitive to stretch. It can sustain being cut, pulverised, even burned but it will complain most volubly when stretched. In the case of brachial neuralgia, sometimes called neuritis of the cervical nerve root, the stretching of the nerve is brought about by the nerve root being distended around the swollen bulk of either a bulging intervertebral disc or a swollen facet joint.

Disc bulges in the neck are rare, for reasons explained on page 62. And it is true to say that disc bulges anywhere in the spine are more inert and less bloody affairs than problems with facet joints. This is simply because discs themselves do not have a blood supply. The fibro-elastic disc material, even when distended by a bulge, is like fingernail and remains relatively remote from the process of normal soft-tissue inflammation. Not so with an inflamed facet joint. By contrast it is red, irritable and swollen, like an inflamed sore throat. In terms of its effect on the spinal nerve, this combination of friction and stretch and inflammation is a potent source of trouble. The nerve itself becomes involved in the inflammatory process and becomes the source of agonising pain.

It is typically described as 'nerve pain' in the arm and depending on which nerve root is involved it is felt in different parts of the arm. Usually there is no pain at all in the neck and you may not even remember what you did to the neck in the first place – nor believe it possible that anything so trivial could be the source of such bother. It is a particularly nasty type of pain, often 'lancinating' in fiery waves down the arm when you move your neck. It is difficult to find any position of the arm where it feels comfortable; sometimes you are only free of it with your hand on top of your head. This is known as an 'antalgic' position and it relieves the pain by taking the nerve fully off the stretch.

These are particularly difficult conditions to treat and are one of the few cases which need adequate rest and anti-inflammatory and muscle-relaxant medication both to dissipate the swelling and to relax the muscle spasm. Only once the acute neuritis has subsided can you commence your own stretches for the neck.

Cervical Spondylosis

For all its flamboyance and grandiose descriptions of pain, brachi-algia of the arm is a relatively rare event. Much more common is a neck that simply doesn't work properly; the grumbling old arthritic neck. Many people complain of this problem though they would be hard pressed to pinpoint what is actually wrong. The neck simply feels stiff to a greater or lesser degree and the most simple mani-festation is pain. It is not a high-pitched screecher sort of pain, although you may well go in and out of the acute episodes described above. It is more a gnawing tiring type of pain and you are aware that your neck is not running properly. Small things can set it off and even if you avoid the full-blown acute neck syndrome you will pass in and out of painful stiff bouts. Your neck never feels quite right; you 'have a neck'. You can hear ominous grinding crackling noises when you move your head. This is the lack of easy-glide in the facet joints, somewhat akin to the squeak of a rusty wheel. You can often feel one or two swollen neck joints the size of marbles. They are 'sweetly' tender to the touch and it is tempting to keep rubbing them to get relief. The muscles running up the back of the neck often feel hard and tense, and they themselves may be an ample source of pain.

This condition is the continuation of the original incident which tweaked one joint in the neck. As described in the Acute Neck section, the facet joint locks up after injury and lays the foundation for general disharmony of the neck as a whole. As the neck finds it harder to keep the head moving, it sprays discord and strain around everywhere and increment by increment movement closes down.

Of course, the simplest manifestation of this is pain. And in the low back, for instance, this is usually the form that trouble takes. But in the neck, other less distinct symptoms can manifest themselves. There may be neck pain but there can also be face pain or a headache, even a migraine. There may be sometimes bizarre, often incomprehensible symptoms like 'grey head', depression, unstable emotions, inability to concentrate, dizziness, ringing in the ears, disturbed hearing, blurred vision, difficulty swallowing, sinusitis or painful teeth . . . just to mention a few.

Simply speaking, you feel the general pain of a neck problem for three distinct reasons. First, the actual soreness from the malfunctioning joint. Like the stiff ankle which fails to work properly, a problem joint in the neck will hurt when it moves. This accounts for the more local pain, right in the neck, and you will dig your fingers into the neck to identify the painful spot.

Then there is referred pain resulting when the irritated joint transmits a far-distant pain to areas using the same nerve supply. This pain spreads out in an amorphous pattern a short distance from the neck – down to the shoulder or up into the head. It is a different mechanism from the pain described in the previous section, where the nerve itself is irritated. Referred pain results from a confusion in the brain over identifying which of the structures sharing a common nerve supply is responsible for causing the pain – rather like the pain of a heart attack being felt in the left upper arm.

Lastly, the pain comes from simple spasm or tightness of the muscles. There are often two components of muscle spasm which contribute to the pain of a problem neck. The first has already been described: the automatic clenching of the muscles at the front and back of the neck. This is only a short-term acute response to a painful stimulus. When the neck feels hurt, the muscles instantly lock up the neck to prohibit any further movement. But like any other muscle in cramp, muscle spasm gives pain. Furthermore, if the neck is going to move out of the acute episode quickly enough, it is important that this state does not last more than a few days.

The second type of spasm is more insidious and long-term and to a degree is related to your own emotional state. It only affects the muscles up the back of the neck (unless that state borders on hysteria) and to a great extent it is under the control of your own volition. It is your own 'elective' muscle spasm, if you like, and its intensity waxes and wanes as you pass in and out of stressful periods. Anxiety, fear, anger, worry; all those things can make you feel worse. They burden your neck with an element of controllable spasm – which you can learn to dispel with relaxation, meditation, breathing control or even hypnosis. In this regard, 'nerves' can often be responsible for a bad neck. They do not cause it in the first place but they may prevent it going away.

WHAT CAN YOU DO ABOUT IT?

These cases outlined above are the extremes. One hopes to catch these problems when the mechanical cause is still in its infancy. The way to thwart the problem in the first place, or rectify it if it has gone beyond that point, is to keep the neck and the thorax fully supple. The rationale is simple: demand maximum participation from the neck and you will watch normal painless movement return.

The bilateral neck angles, where the neck joins the shoulders, are particularly at risk since it is here that the delicate spinal stalk peers out of the thorax like a tortoise's neck out of its shell. It is right here too, that the shoulder girdle hangs itself off the spine like a weighty coat-hanger; lashing itself to the spine by a bulky criss-cross of musculature which not only pulls the neck back erect but also controls the shoulders and wields the arms. All this can make for a very bunched-up area, especially if tension is part of everyday life.

73

EXERCISE 1

The Elbow Lift

1 Stand with your feet squarely on the floor and clasp the hands, interlacing the fingers right down at the web.

2 Place these clenched fists fully under your jaw so that as little a part of the hands as possible protrudes past the line of your chin.

3 Keeping your elbows pinched together, raise the elbow tips in an arc out from your chest and point them up as high to the ceiling as you can, inhaling as you go. At the same time, tip your head back on your shoulders with your fists reinforcing the backwards angulation of the neck where it joins the thoracic spine.

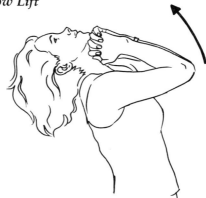

4 Relax and bring your elbows back down to your chest, exhaling as you go.

5 Repeat six times.

74

EXERCISE 2

The Head Clasp

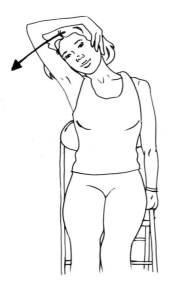

1 Sit squarely on a chair with your feet comfortably on the floor.

2 Place your left hand, palm down, under your left buttock so that you are sitting on it.

3 Tilting (not turning) your head to the right, bring your right hand up and over your head.

4 Spread the fingers of your right hand wide and cup as far down the left-hand side of the face as it will reach. The weight of your right forearm will be lying along the upper left aspect of your crown, reinforcing the right angulation of the head.

5 Hold for 15 seconds and release.

6 Repeat three times and then change sides and repeat another four times.

EXERCISE 3

The Plough

This is the same as the sixth exercise for the thoracic spine. You will need a robust pillow and a small stool.

1 Position the stool about forty-five centimetres (eighteen inches) away from the pillow on the floor.

2 Lie on your back on the floor with the pillow positioned crossways under your shoulders and your head free on the floor.

3 Raise both legs up and swing them up and over your head so that your feet rest on the stool behind your head. Make this movement smooth not jerky. Support your bottom with your hands (arms bent at the elbows) and hold this position for as long as you can – up to 5 minutes if possible – relaxed and breathing evenly all the time. The pillow should be positioned to allow a step-down at the point where the thorax becomes the neck and this spares the neck from too much pushing under. The more uncomfortable the neck feels, the higher the pillow step-down. You will find the exercise hard to do at first; a pull on the neck and hard to breathe, but even holding it for 15 seconds helps.

You will feel a mixed sensation of stretch and pain in your middle back which will be relieved only by relaxing into the pain and gently breathing through it.

4 As you practise this you will find that you can progress the movement further by removing the stool and allowing your knees to bend down on to your forehead.

EXERCISE 4

The Swastika

1 Lie on your front on the floor with your head turned to the right.
2 Bring your left arm out at ninety degrees and also bend your left elbow by ninety degrees. Place the palm of this hand on the floor above your head.
3 Bring your right arm out to make a right angle with your shoulder and also bend the elbow ninety degrees but this time have the palm upwards so your right hand rests out by the side of your right hip. One arm will now be crooked up, the other crooked down. The right arm will now be fully internally rotated at the shoulder whereas the left arm will be fully externally rotated at the shoulder.

4 Bring your left leg up in the same way as you did your left arm: the upper leg at ninety degrees to the body and the knee bent by ninety degrees. The right leg remains straight on the floor. Hold the position for at least 2 minutes. You will feel a stretch all through your neck and across your shoulders into your upper torso.
5 After 2 minutes release and change sides. Repeat the exercise in the opposite direction.

NB Make sure your head is always turned towards the hand you cannot see.

EXERCISE 5

The Tipped Head and Neck Twist

The main problem with this exercise is finding a soft and low enough surface from which to start. Perhaps the best arrangement is a set of about four sturdy sofa cushions piled on the floor making a height of about thirty centimetres (twelve inches) when compressed.

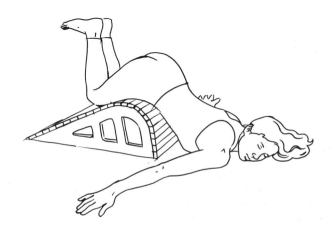

1 Kneel on the floor and begin to lower yourself by your arms over the stack of cushions, sliding forwards so that the chest/higher abdominal area passes on to the floor.

2 Turn your head to the right and complete the lowering process so that your left cheek and left side of your face presses against the floor. Once your face is on the floor you may have to get purchase with your toes to push yourself further forwards over the cushions so that the downwards slope of your upper back gently spears your face into the floor.

3 Place both arms out from your body and hold the position for 1 minute, then withdraw and relax. Repeat once.

4 Repeat twice facing the other direction.

Chapter Eight

THE SHOULDERS

WHAT IS THE SHOULDER?

The shoulder is where the arm meets the torso. It is a very mobile joint which allows multi-directional freedom of the arm. In theory it is a ball and socket joint although in practice it is hardly that. The ball is there all right; a large round knob at the top of the humerus, the shaft of the upper arm. But the socket bears little resemblance to its counterpart in the hip. Instead of the head being deeply encapsulated in a bony pocket, as the thigh bone is into the pelvis, the socket of the shoulder joint is a shallow little saucer, about the size of a 10 pence piece. The top of the head of the humerus nestles under a joint made by the collar bone or clavicle at the front and the bony ledge of the shoulder blade or scapula at the back. This forms the acromio-clavicular joint which can often be ruptured by force upwards through the long shaft of the humerus. The presence of the acromium and the clavicle creates a slight hood over the head of the humerus which provides some stability for the shoulder, especially in generous movements where the arm lifts up high above the head.

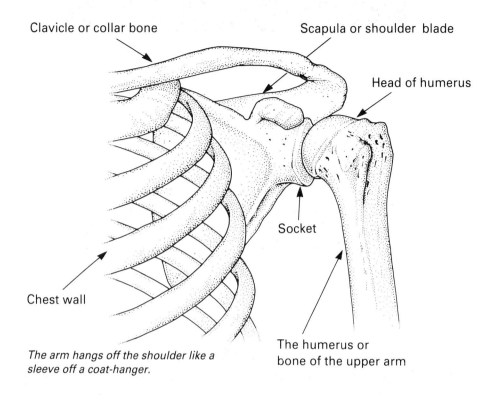

Clavicle or collar bone

Scapula or shoulder blade

Head of humerus

Socket

Chest wall

The arm hangs off the shoulder like a sleeve off a coat-hanger.

The humerus or bone of the upper arm

HOW DOES THE SHOULDER WORK?

The arm fastens to the socket known as the glenoid cavity, an outermost projection of the scapula. It is loosely held in place by the baggy capsule of the shoulder, so that the arm hangs off the shoulder girdle like the sleeve of a coat off a coat-hanger. The round head of the humerus hangs gently against the shallow socket, and skids and glides around on it as the arm moves. But this base or fixing for the mobile arm is far from being a rigid structure. The scapula itself has its own freedom as well, which adds another dimension of freedom to the hand. Considering the human hand also has the added benefit of the opposing thumb which makes it so expert at manipulating objects and doing precision finger work, it is particularly ideal that it is given so much freedom by both the sloppy shoulder joint and the mobility of the scapula. In its role as a mobile base for all arm movement, the scapula scoots all around the back and the side of the chest wall. This provides a lot of background mobility, even before the arm in the socket makes its contribution. You can demonstrate this for yourself. By keeping your arm stiff at the shoulder and just manoeuvring your shoulder blade, it is apparent that there is a lot of useful movement at the hand.

The arm-in-the-socket movement at the shoulder is controlled by a collar of short muscles which spans the joint space and operates the multi-directional hinge. The muscles wrap around the head of the humerus in close interweaving harmony and by shortening as they contract, rather like puppet strings shortening, they operate the lever of the arm. Like all things in nature, this feat is remarkable. The arm is extremely long and ungainly in relation to the length and strength of its controlling muscles. This means that all these muscles act at a significant mechanical disadvantage, something which has important implications in the development of dys-function of the shoulder.

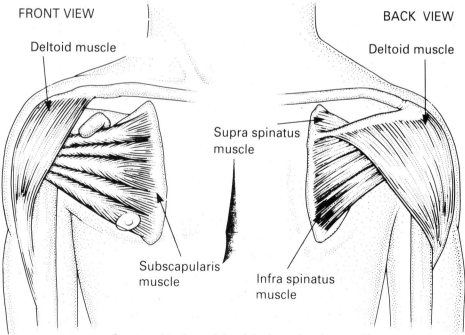

Compared to the weight of the lever they have to lift (the arm) the muscles of the shoulder are seemingly dwarf to the task.

The collar of muscles, known as the rotator cuff of muscles, has a secondary function. It hugs the head of the humerus close to the scapula and so reinforces the role of the capsule in holding the head into the socket. This rotating cuff of muscles gives the shoulder joint its stability; it stops the shoulder falling out of joint. You only have to see how vexing a recurring dislocation of the shoulder can be to appreciate fully the role that these muscles usually play in keeping the shoulder stable. Recurring dislocation is usually the legacy of past traumatic injury which has left the binding musculature stretched so that the joint repeatedly falls out.

WHAT ARE THE ACCESSORY MOVEMENTS AT THE SHOULDER?

Like all joints and joint-complexes, the presence of accessory mobility is essential for streamlined performance. This is particularly true for the shoulder. Here, accessory freedom not only lends the joint a youthful dexterity but it also performs a vital role in enhancing the action of muscles of the shoulder. It influences the power of the arm. This all goes back to the unwieldly length of the arm and the slenderness of the muscle cover. Whereas the arm may be some sixty centimetres (twenty-four inches) in length – and I don't know how heavy – every single muscle operating the arm at the shoulder hinge is diminutive by comparison. This is quite unlike the leg, for example, where the hamstrings and the quadriceps bulk is mammoth, running the entire length of the thigh and vast enough to grab in cupped hands. The muscles of the upper arm are short and slight and, except for the deltoid muscle, almost impossible to identify under the skin. Whereas both the hamstrings and the quadriceps (which bend and straighten the knee) enjoy a mechanical advantage because of their ratio of power to the length of the lever they operate, the arm muscles at the shoulder work against great odds. The length of the lever in the arm that they have to pick up, in comparison to their own bulk and the spread from which they take strength, makes it almost seem hopeless at the start. None of them is more than several centimetres in length and they work at impossible angles to get the arm to act.

If these small muscles are to have any chance at all of making the heavy arm work, it is imperative that there is plenty of latitude for the arm head to manoeuvre in the socket so that the muscles can operate at their most advantageous angle to pull. The head must be able to shuffle about on the lip of the socket so that it can take up the best position for each specific operating muscle to work.

Accessory freedom at the shoulder provides just this sort of movement. Take the arm going up over the head, for example. When this happens, it is crucial that there is a small preparatory movement of the head gliding *down* on the socket. This action is brought about by other muscles (how, for the moment, is not important) but its contribution to the overall grand movement is that it puts the prime mover muscle in its best position to act; more specifically, it puts it on the stretch. This improves the angle of pull for that muscle's action which dramatically enhances its ease of performance. The arm floats up effortlessly above the head.

All major arm movements require this sort of preparatory positioning. Using the analogy of the rope and pulley arrangement, optimal line of pull is the essential ingredient if the movement is to be as easy as possible. Without such a thing, the muscles are forced to labour at difficult angles of pull which reduces their efficiency and requires increased effort. Muscle strain is the most apparent outcome with stiffness and loss of elasticity the result. But there are also more specific manifestations such as tendonitis, caused by the increased friction of one muscle against its neighbours, which will be discussed later.

Continuing with the example of raising your arm above your head, I will explain how – if you did the opposite preparatory movement – you would put yourself at a disadvantage. The muscles which lift the arm over the head run from the top of the scapula to the top of the head of the humerus. By shortening with a muscle contraction, they lever the arm up. If the head were to ride *up* instead of down preparatory to the movement, these muscles would find themselves in a slackened or lengthened state, a point from which they find it difficult to shorten adequately to pull the lever of the arm around. Like the villain in the movies who is forced to drop the knife by having his wrist forced under, if the muscles are put into their fully slackened position it is difficult for them to achieve a powerful contraction. The gangster drops the knife because the flexor muscles which curl the fingers around the knife are powerfully discommoded by being put in a position where they are as slack as flaccid elastic, and cannot contract properly.

Whether you bring your arm up above the head to comb your hair, out from the side to slip your arm in the sleeve of a coat, up behind your back when towelling your back dry, or simply bring your hand up to your mouth when eating, the head of the humerus needs to adopt a position on the socket of the glenoid cavity. The head must be loose, free to slide forwards and back, up and down as well as out away from the socket if it is to be able to position itself effectively for the vast variety of arm movements. These are the accessory movements of the shoulder.

83

How Does the Shoulder Go Wrong?

Simple weakness of the upper arms, often brought about by poor posture coupled with bad habits, can be the factor which squeezes out the accessory function of a shoulder joint. The key to this is the fundamentally different nature of the type of muscles which operate the scapula as distinct from the arm. The muscles which operate the scapula are known as 'postural' muscles. Their power of contraction is of low intensity but of long duration; they are at work for all the hours that we are up and about. They act along with all the other anti-gravity muscles to keep the skeleton upright and standing. The rotator cuff muscles of the shoulder-proper are different. They only act when you want your arm to do something deliberate and purposeful such as swatting a fly or conducting a symphony orchestra. These are known as 'phasic' muscles because they sweep into action with explosive effort to perform a specific task and then, once the job is done, relax back and rest.

If these phasic muscles are simply weak, the first stone is laid in the mosaic of dysfunction. As strenuous arm work comes along, the poor power of the arms is compensated for by gross movements of the scapula. This will cause a progressive domination of shoulder blade activity to compensate for weakness at the arm-shoulder hinge. Complications multiply at this point, with the acting out of one of the fundamental neurophysiological tenets: overactivity of the postural group causes automatic inhibition of the phasic group. In simple language: the upper arm itself becomes weak; its finer more articulate function becomes swamped and obliterated by the clumsy grosser movements of the shoulder blade. The latter overrides the former.

This unbalanced effort is known in clinical circles as 'reverse scapulo-humeral rhythm'. Most of us demonstrate this to a subtle degree, although it is an anomaly of movement which is not easy to pick up. To the untrained eye it only becomes noticeable when the arm is involved in strenuous effort. Then, the actions seem to involve an immense amount of burly shoulder girdle activity with a lot of hunching and bunching of the shoulders to wrest things about. It seems impossible to use the arm in a pure, graceful hinging way, to wit the armwork of a ballerina.

I, for example, am very weak here, as most women are. When I try to lift a heavy suitcase, say, I am only too aware of how awkward it is. I have to heave it off the floor using both hands and the whole shoulder girdle. I put my whole shoulder to it, just to yank it up. I don't seem to have the simple strength in my arms to pluck it from the floor and carry it. And if I do get it up, I drag it, clattering against my legs as I stumble over it and drop it a few steps further on. No wonder I hate travelling. There is no chance of my lifting it like the muscle-man, who picks it up in a seemingly effortless manner and trots away with it. He holds the case high and out from his body with one hand, steering a steady course as if it were an inconsequential lightweight. I can always tell on the movies, incidentally, when the actors are carrying suitcases which are meant to be stuffed full but are in fact empty. No shoulder bunching and heaving for them.

They whirl the cases around free in the air like the flying horses on a carousel. Far too easy to be real.

Back to shoulders. In the early stages simple dysfunction is not painful, just awkward like it is for me. You become accustomed to not having the power in your upper arm and for the most part you unwittingly call in the scapula to compensate or if you're like me you kick the suitcase along with your foot. But the relative inactivity of the arm at the shoulder sets a chain of events in motion; the progressive dysfunction of the shoulder complex. By degrees the muscles of the socket-hinge contract down and become short and tight – and more ineffectual. As they become tight they also become weak, and this combination sets the stage for speedy despair.

The simple weakness and tightness of the muscles makes them vulnerable. If you make a chance movement which demands their action they are too feeble to make an honest attempt. As you lean over the car seat, for example, to grab your briefcase from the back, you feel a nasty twang in the shoulder. The arm is too weak to do the movement and so you have strained one of the muscles, the initial act in introducing subtle discord to the joint. Inelasticity from lack of full active use of this musculature can result in the same thing happening: lack of stretch means that jarring or wrenching of the joint becomes an easy thing to do. That joint which should be able to swing loosely becomes an easy target to annoy. The most trivial of actions can do it; the bus jerking as you are hanging there on the roof strap, or catching the strap of your handbag on a door handle, or a child hanging off one arm.

One by one a chance awkward action at just the angle to yank a tight and unforgiving muscle, then the muscle is hurt. Automatic spasm of the surrounding muscles is set up, to hold the arm still and to guard against further unwanted movement. This is how the problem snowballs. One muscle in spasm introduces further unsettling discord into the working system. It goes on to seed further dysfunction; as the problem becomes more widespread all the muscles in the plaited complex are injured and stiffen in turn. The poor shoulder is eventually unable to make any spontaneous movements without more jarring and more pain. The domino effect has roped them all in and you have your frozen shoulder: a general closing down of all-round movement of the shoulder.

THE COMMON DISORDERS OF THE SHOULDER

The common degenerative disorders all relate directly either to too little accessory movement – the 'frozen' shoulder; or too much accessory movement – dislocation of the joint.

Frozen shoulder

This is the commonest acquired affliction of the shoulder joint. It is where the shoulder joint progressively loses freedom and becomes stiff and painful. All movements become difficult but especially awkward is getting a coat on, doing up a bra and getting a brush to the top of the head. The problem usually comes on insidiously. Usually you cannot recall anything you might have done to start it all. Occasionally I hear a tale of you twisting your arm over the car seat to pull up the back-door button or a yank of another kind with the arm in an awkward position. Then there may have been a momentary sharp tweak of pain which seemed to fade with a bit of rubbing and soothing, after which the shoulder became unsettled.

Whatever the case, whether there is pain or no pain, severe cases of frozen shoulder reveal a severely dysfunctional unit. There is virtually no movement at all at the shoulder hinge, all activity of the arm coming from the pure scapula movement. All accessory movement of the head of the humerus on the socket has been obliterated. Any movement of the arm involves marked humping of the shoulder as the scapula heaves about. When you to try to raise your arm above your head, the whole forequarter lifts and comes up towards your ear. From behind your whole body swings back in an attempt to give the arm more elevation. When you try to move your arm out from the side of your body, you only move it a few degrees before you see the scapula poke out from the side of your chest and web the skin up like a disabled wing. In all movements, effort is the overriding feature. You try to assist the arm with your other hand, even to get your hand to the door handle.

You feel the pain in the upper third of the outer aspect of your upper arm as a deep, gnawing pain. You want to rub and squeeze your arm and you often think that you have a 'muscle problem' under the site of the pain. Unguarded movement is a curse; it can send a searing wave of agony through your arm. Sleeping may be a problem since this shoulder does not like taking the weight of the body lying on it overnight.

Severe cases of frozen shoulder can take up to two years to resolve, and there is one school of orthopaedic opinion which says no amount of physical treatment can help. Severe debility, of course, is not as common as all the lesser degrees of a grumbling disorder, en route to becoming the fully-fledged disorder. These are much more common and manifest themselves in all age groups, whereas severe frozen shoulder usually restricts itself to the over-50s age group.

If someone like me examines one of these severe shoulders, we are always met with the same clear findings: an arm which is tightly bound to its mobile base – the scapula. All accessory movements are missing and when we attempt to get gliding movements of the head across the top of the socket we are met with springy resistance. The shoulder itself often feels more bony or pointy, as the muscle bulk around the head has wasted away. The shoulder itself appears to be pinned forwards, so that when you lie down on your back the shoulder and upper arm perch up in front of the rest of the body instead of lying back flat, relaxed and floppy against the bed. But more importantly, when we attempt to take your arm gently above your head there comes a point, depending on how restricted the complex is, when the shoulder blade comes along too. In less severe cases due to general lack of fitness this will not be until the last few degrees of elevation of the arm, when your upper arm is nearing your ear. But at this point you feel pain. The whole shoulder feels tight uncomfortable and vulnerable – especially if your arm is taken out a bit, away from your head. This manoeuvre is substantially stressing the tight shoulder joint union.

Tendonitis

This is usually the result of repetitive use of the arm in one particular pattern. It is inflammation of one tendon, a condition which appears to be a further development of an afflicted tight shoulder. When the head of the humerus is too closely bound to the shoulder blade to permit vital 'internal manoeuvrability' the strain soon tells if one muscle (and its tendon) is subjected to the same action over and over again. Swimming is a good example, especially freestyle or crawl which involves the arm in coming up and over the head with every stroke. A disadvantaged angle of pull resulting from poor accessory freedom within the joint subjects the tendon of the prime mover muscle to much increased wear and tear. Repetitive use, especially if the action is a meagre one, soon sets up friction between this muscle and its neighbours which leads on to chafing and even fraying of the tendon. With swimmers however, there is some evidence another factor contributes to their supraspinatus tendonitis. It is thought that the overdeveloped bulk of the supraspinatus muscle means that it cannot thread itself neatly under the bony shelf which over-hangs the top of the shoulder (the clavicle), and that the rolling head of the humerus pinches the muscle between itself and that shelf. The tendonitis is caused not only by the labouring of that tendon's action but also by the tendon actually being abraded between the two bones during the action. Inflammation sets in.

With supraspinatus tendonitis, the pain is acute. It is a much hotter problem than the chronic smouldering one of frozen shoulder. You usually go to your doctor because you experience a 'painful arc' of movement when moving your arm up above your head. You start the movement well enough but at about forty-five degrees out from your side there is an excruciating patch of pain as the muscle moves through the part of its range where the tendon is most taxed. Beyond this point, from about ninety degrees on, the movement is painless again. The painful arc comes on as the inflamed tendon squeezes under the clavicle at the tip of the shoulder; once it has passed under, the rest of the action in raising the arm above the head is painless. To avoid this searing arc of pain you will unwittingly do all sorts of trick manoeuvres, even help it with your other hand, to spare using the inflamed tendon. Hunching your shoulder and undulating your arm, you will try to 'go around' the problem as you lift the arm up above your head.

WHAT CAN YOU DO ABOUT IT?

Correction of these shoulder problems requires the loosening of the head-to-socket union. Simply speaking, this undoes the chain of events outlined above. It restores some space to the joint so that the head has room to manoeuvre. Then the head of the humerus resumes its vital gliding function so that not only can your shoulder begin to absorb shock, it can also position itself adequately so that its musculature can operate optimally. The yoga stretches in the final section of this chapter will do all this for you. If you begin early enough you will prevent the problem from starting but even if you are in trouble, they will slowly turn the problem round. If your shoulder is severely debilitated you will not be able to start straightaway on the following yoga stretches; they are too robust and will cause your shoulder to clam up even more. At this stage you must do the gentlest pendular movements, swinging your arm like an elephant's trunk. This alone several times a day starts the process off. The simple weight of the arm is enough to get some of the initial distraction of the head off the rim of the socket and start everything moving.

The universal first step to be taken in the treatment of these problems is to release the tightness between the arm and the scapula. If I were to treat you in my clinic I might initially mobilise the ball in the socket at the tip of your shoulder myself but quite quickly I would expect you to begin your own yoga stretches.

EXERCISE 1

The Shoulder Hang

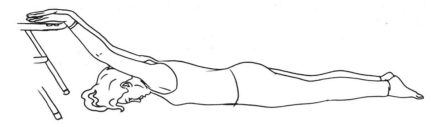

You will need a kitchen chair for this.
1 Lie face down on the floor with the chair about twenty centimetres (eight inches) beyond your head.
2 Lift one arm at a time and place the flat of each hand on the seat of the chair. (You may have to push the chair further away if you find the front edge is digging into your forearms.)

3 Straighten both arms at the elbows and drop your head through your shoulders down towards the floor. You will feel the pull diagonally up under your chest and under to the front of your shoulders.
4 Hang there for at least 60 seconds then rest for a while before repeating twice more.

EXERCISE 2

The Backwards Shoulder

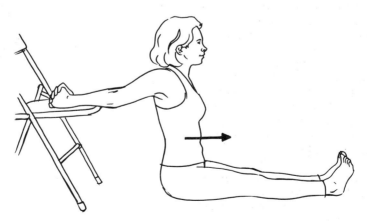

You will need a kitchen chair for this.
1 Sit on the floor with your legs stretched out in front of you and the chair about twenty centimetres (eight inches) behind you.

2 Lift one arm and place it on the chairseat behind you.

3 Bring your other arm back to the chairseat and interlace your fingers. Try to bring the heels of the hands together as you clasp your hands.

4 Straighten both arms at the elbow and also straighten your spine. Do not allow your chest to cave in but thrust it forwards and try to hollow your low back. You may find it easier at first to sit on a pillow as this will lower the relative height of the chair.

5 Hold the position for 60 seconds then relax. Repeat two more times.

EXERCISE 3

The Praying Shoulder Stretch

You will need to use a piece of furniture or structure with a flat surface at hip height (a broad windowsill is ideal).

1 Place your feet about ten centimetres (four inches) apart and bend your hips at right angles while leaning your elbows on the windowsill.

2 Place your elbows on the surface just wide enough apart to allow your head to drop through the gap.

3 From this position take your hands above your head with the palms together as if in the praying position, the elbows making a ninety-degree angle. Do not allow your spine to hump up.

4 Hold this position for 2 minutes then release. When it comes to disengaging from the stretch you will find it easier to duck out of the position by bringing one leg forwards and bending its knee.

5 With practice you will be able to progress this exercise further by bending the elbows and dropping the hands, the palms still pressed together, down on to your upper back. Hold this position for another 30 seconds and release.

91

EXERCISE 4

The 'T' Shape

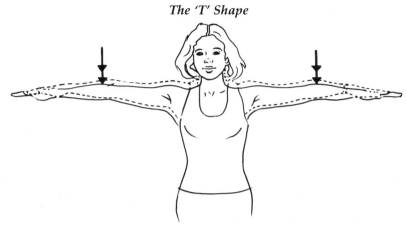

This is a simple exercise but hard to do well.

1 Stand upright with your feet five centimetres (two inches) apart and your hands by your sides.

2 Slowly raise both arms until they are exactly horizontal, fingertips level with your shoulders.

3 Maintain this position without hunching the shoulders for at least 1 minute. You'll be surprised how difficult it is to keep this crisp T-shape of your body. 'Energise' your arms by keeping them straight and your fingers thrust straight out so you sense energy leaving the fingertips. Make a deliberate effort to depress your shoulder girdle while keeping your fingertips up.

4 Lower your arms and let them hang loose while you breathe deeply to recuperate.

5 Repeat twice more, making sure you do not hunch your shoulders at any time.

6 With practice you will be able to hold this position for 2 minutes. It's a long time.

EXERCISE 5

The Rolling Pin Stretch

You will need a kitchen chair and a rolling pin or an umbrella for this.

1 Kneel on your knees in front of the chair.

2 Hold the rolling pin with your palms upwards then lean forwards and rest your weight on your elbows on the chairseat. (The elbows and the hands should all be shoulder-width apart.)

3 Bend your elbows to ninety degrees and let your head drop down through your arms.

4 Hold this position for 2 minutes, breathing slowly and regularly all the time to help stay relaxed. This is a

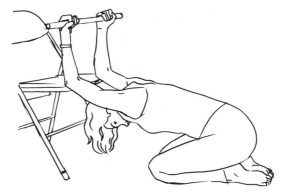

painful exercise and your muscles will want to tense up. Don't fight against yourself: keep your eyes closed, your breathing rhythmic and let your head float away.

5 With practice you will be able to progress this exercise by taking your hands further apart along the rolling pin.

EXERCISE 6

The Behind Your Back Twist

You will need a kitchen chair for this.
1 Sit on the chair and lift your right arm straight above your head.
2 Keeping your upper arm as close to your ear as possible, bend your elbow and let your right hand flop down behind your right shoulder.
3 Turning your left arm inwards at the shoulder, take the left hand up high behind your back. If you can, link hands behind your back. If they don't reach you can trail a strap from your top hand down to the bottom one so that the hands are linked by the strap. Keep your right elbow pointing high up towards the ceiling and hold the position for 30 seconds before releasing.
4 Repeat twice more then change sides and repeat three times on the other side.

EXERCISE 7

The Broomstick Stretch

You will need a long stick, perhaps a walking stick, for this. If you haven't got one you could use a broomstick or an umbrella.

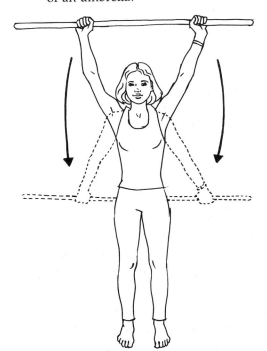

1 Stand upright and grasp the stick with the hands about eighty centimetres (thirty-two inches) apart, palms downwards. Begin with the stick held horizontally across the front of your thighs.

2 Lift the stick upwards, over your head and then down behind your back so it rests on your bottom. The important point is to keep the stick horizontal as it goes over your head. You will need to resist the temptations to allow one elbow to bend or one arm to lead the movement. Your fingertips will tend to pull away from the stick so keep a firm grip.

3 Reverse the movement to bring the stick over and back to its starting point.

4 Repeat several times in one generous sweeping movement.

5 As you practice you can progress this exercise by bringing the hands in closer along the stick.

Chapter Nine

THE
ELBOWS

WHAT IS THE ELBOW?

The elbow bends the arm into a lever of manageable length. At first sight it looks like a simple hinge but if you look more closely you see that it is not. There is a twisting subtlety in the working forearm which converts the arm from being a relatively clumsy robot-like lever (which from a functional point of view is pretty useless) into the remarkable and graceful tool that it is. This is brought about by the two parallel bones of the forearm revolving around each other, carrying the hand along too. There is a swivelling action of the two bones, rather like using chopsticks. The mobile chopstick is the radius which revolves around the ulna, the fixed chopstick. Combined with the dextrous fingers and the thumb in action all the way round, you can see what a devastatingly effective apparatus it is.

HOW DOES THE ELBOW WORK?

It is the twirl and the flourish of the hinging arm which make all the difference. They invest the arm with that peculiarly fluid quality of motion which makes it look 'living' as opposed to synthesised. We

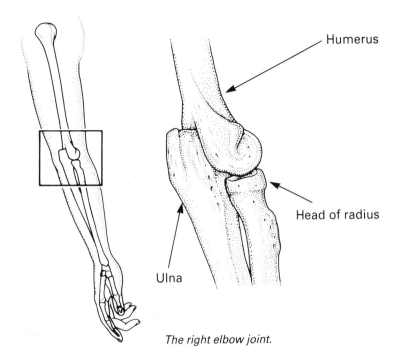

The right elbow joint.

see a perfect amalgam of several-movements-in-one in all animal movements but perhaps never better than at the lower end of the human arm. By contrast, you only have to think of the way a doll's arm moves up and down, across and back, with never a hope of anything useful at the hand. The twist adds an extra dimension by making a three-dimensional movement out of two. Imagine a damsel plucking a daisy and bringing it around under her nose to smell it and you'll see streamlined human movement with that languid dreamy curling quality to it.

The hand is brought around by the radius – the thumbside bone of the forearm – as it spins lengthwise on its axis. The head of the radius at the top end of the bone fits snugly against the ulna just below the elbow crease. The radial head is held in place by a loose collar of ligament running around the neck of the radius and attaching back to the ulna. As the radius spins, the hand by being attached to the bottom of the radius is flopped over. At all times the ulna (on

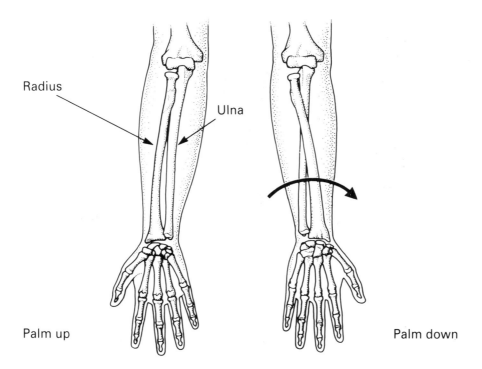

Radius

Ulna

Palm up

Palm down

As the hand pronates, or turns the palm over, the radius swivels on its axis and

the two bones cross. The ulna hinges with the humerus to bend the elbow.

the underside of the forearm) remains fairly static. Its main role is to connect with the upper arm at the hinge joint of the elbow.

You can make the two bones dance around each other and the radius bring the hand over by holding the crease of one elbow with the other hand and turning the hand from a palm-up position right through 180 degrees to palm-down. For more practical purposes useful movement at the elbow involves two actions: the hinging of the elbow along with this swivelling of the forearm. Take the movement of bringing a fork up to the mouth, for example. What makes the movement so sensationally accurate, so that you don't get tomato sauce all over your face, is the ability to rotate the fork right around and direct it smack into the mouth. Just watch a toddler trying to master this manoeuvre and you'll see what a complex series of movements it is. The rotation action refines the hard-nosed elements of the other actions and hones them into bull's-eye accuracy with subtlety and precision. We then crawl through space with maximum purpose and minimum effort as the superbly smooth and dynamic machines that we are.

Rotation is a crucial action as it allows us to address objects side on. This means we can get better access to things by getting closer in. For example, this might be by bending down to pick up a carton from the floor or it might be the fine hand co-ordination needed to play the violin. Rotation is particularly important to the human arm because so much uniquely human effort is to be found in the precise movements at the fingertips. When threading a needle, we need to be able to get right there. The arm must place the fingertips exactly where they have to go. This skill, in combination with the bonus of our opposing thumb technique, makes for even greater effectiveness and dexterity of upper limb activity.

WHAT ARE THE ACCESSORY MOVEMENTS OF THE ELBOW?

The important accessory movement at the elbow is the spin of the radial head in its ligamentous collar at the top end of the ulna. If it is free to go, it will let the long shaft of the radius rotate on its axis and bring the hand around with it. The looser the collar – called the collateral ligament – the looser the movement. If the movements of our forearms start to become jerky and less fluid, it is because the elbow has tightened up and choked the freedom of the radial head. There will be a rapid drop-off in the invisible background element of twist in the forearm and a subtle deficiency in the elbow's more 'obvious' function. If the background contribution is poor, the overall performance will be poor – tomato sauce all down the front. The reverse is also true: the more unimpeded the subtle rotation element, the more proficient your general performance.

Coarser movements (in this case, the bending and the straightening of the elbow) can survive a more marked relative loss of freedom than finer ones before useful function will suffer. This is because we have little use for the extremes in range that the large joints offer. For example, we never use the elbow bunched in tight to the chest; though in truth lack of full straightening does pose greater problems – when reaching out to open a door, for example, or bearing weight on a straight arm. Any flaws here will be immediately apparent in their nuisance value.

Flaws in the rotation element are far harder to detect although signs may be present. The business of hand writing is a good example. Even the slightest impairment in the freedom of the two bones in your forearm to revolve around one another will cause the quality of your writing to suffer. It happens to us all as we get older. The spontaneous fluidity goes. So graphically charted by the course of the pen across the page, the writing reveals itself as less rounded, smaller, wobbly, even crotchety – in short, the hand of an older scribe.

How Do Elbows Go Wrong?

The elbows are a better example than most of how a joint can be seriously disturbed by imperfect muscle parity. The group of muscles which clothes the uppermost aspect of the forearm are responsible for lifting the hand back when it is lying palm-down on the surface of a table. In its more functional role it does things like turning a door knob (always a backwards movement) or grabbing at the handle of a briefcase. These are very specific and powerful movements of the wrist and they also tend to be repetitive. The group of muscles which does this action – all lumped together under the name of 'the common extensors' of the wrist – attaches itself to the bone over a very small area on the inside of the bony bump we can feel on the outside of the elbow. Almost as if it were a defect of Creation, this very able and frequently used group of muscles, instead of having the tissues which attach it to the bone spread over a wide area to lessen the force transmitted to the bone when the muscles contract, has nothing of the sort. Instead, the area of attachment is tiny and with frequent use of the hand in certain actions this can cause havoc. If the actions are forcible as well as repetitive in nature, a tugging action tends to pull the muscle off the bone and in no time at all inflammation sets in.

In this case it is hard to say what came first, the chicken or the egg. Did the joint get tight first and cause the muscles to pull awkwardly or did the yanking of the muscles so jangle up the joint that it could no longer function properly? In most cases, I think the latter.

The elbow is by nature a very tight joint. So much so, that when a nasty trauma like a fracture or dislocation afflicts the elbow the medical team must get in there without delay to release the build-up of blood and fluid trapped inside the joint. If it isn't drained, the pressure of the encapsulated blood will strangle the nerves and other blood vessels passing through the joint and the result can be devastating: a useless and unsightly claw hand, something which is easily avoided and therefore fortunately rarely seen.

The natural tightness of the joint means that it has a diminished ability to ride out the normal jolts of life. If we then add to its inherent tightness the jarring of over-zealous and repetitive armwork, we quickly take the joint to the limits of its tolerance. If the joint is repeatedly jarred it adopts the defence mechanism of clenching itself to help ride out the blows. This rapidly makes things worse. One memorable wrench is usually the first step in the process. This initial shock immediately closes down the joint and then it is even more poorly equipped to cope with the continued overbearing action of one muscle group. It keeps on getting knocked by incidental movement and this sets up a vicious cycle. The more the condition deteriorates, the less forgiving the joint becomes and the more it gets hurt.

When we physiotherapists examine these joints we find their function very disturbed. To the casual observer the elbow seems to move reasonably well, but it doesn't close up. It usually lacks full extension (straightening) as well as full twist of the forearm (especially at extremes of flexion and extension). Subtle degrees of inward and outward angulation at the elbow are also missing.

THE COMMON DISORDERS OF THE ELBOW
Tennis Elbow

There is no function more vexatious to the forearm than the backhand shot at tennis: that backwards slash at the ball while holding a heavy and shock-resistant racquet. A ripple or more accurately a thud of shock-wave is transmitted through the clenched forearm to the origin of the muscle – the point where the tendon glues itself to the bone. This is a shock and what's more a shock which is repeated over and over again every time your backhand connects with another of those zinging balls. Each savage wrench causes microscopic tearing of these fibres where they adhere to the bone. There is local oozing of fluid, local swelling and soon enough you have a 'hot spot' in your skeletal system; a painful elbow. Tennis elbow.

In clinical practice, you all arrive at our surgeries with the same sort of picture, though tennis need not have been the cause. You will often be holding the elbow as you explain things, as if proffering an unruly problem. Sometimes you find yourself absentmindedly rubbing the painful spot which gives some relief. Your arm is acutely sensitive over the outer knob of the elbow and if you knock the arm, which once it is sore you seem to do all the time, it is agony. You drop everything and clutch it with the other hand until it feels better. Even to be brushed past in the street can make you stop and draw breath. At worst, you cannot even turn a key in the door without gasping with pain.

The background pain is usually felt as a broad band down the front of the forearm, sometimes to the wrist. You actively demur at the prospect of having to shake hands, since that is particularly painful. Indeed one of my patients claims he got his tennis elbow after joining a large legal firm, when he spent the first two weeks shaking hands with other partners. In this typically male domain the more macho the handshake, the more leveraged the balance of control.

WHAT CAN YOU DO ABOUT IT?

So what is the way around it? The answer is to loosen the joint as a whole so that it can pull apart and accommodate a normal-enough wrench as it passes through the arm. By improving all-round joint laxity the normal elasticity of the soft tissues binding the joint will absorb the trauma, rather than jerk and cause the extensor group to rip away from the bone. In all but the severest cases, this is the way we manage the problem. Only as a last resort do we call for injecting steroids (such as cortisone) and local anaesthetic into the hot spot. Incidentally, even though cortisone is used it cannot alone usually rectify the problem. In the short-term it will dampen the inflammation but in the long-term, if joint play is not restored, the problem will resurface.

EXERCISE 1

The Forearm Stretch

1 Kneel on your hands and knees on the floor. Position your knees directly under your hips and your hands directly under your shoulders.
2 Turn both hands inwards so that your fingers point directly back towards your knees. This fully twists your shoulders in.
3 With your elbows completely straight, rock gently back on your knees and feel the intensity of the stretch running down your forearm and under your wrist. Hold this position for 15 seconds then gently rock forwards to your starting position.
4 Release your hands and then turn them outwards right round the other way so that the fingers point straight back towards the knees. This

twists the shoulders outwards. Again, remember to keep the elbows straight.

5 Rock gently back on your knees and hold this position for 15 seconds.

You will feel the pull down the front of the forearms.

6 Alternate the stretches and do each one four times.

EXERCISE 2

The Forearm Twist

You will need a kitchen chair for this exercise.

1 Sit comfortably in a chair, extend both arms straight out horizontally in front of you with your hands back to back.

2 Bring your right hand over your left hand so that the palms touch. Interlace your fingers right down to the web.

3 Keeping your hands locked together, bring them down and towards you, in and under through to the chest and then up and out through the space between your arms and stretch them out horizontally again. You will find that this

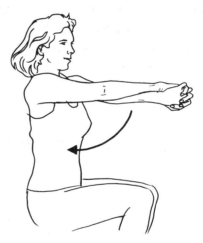

causes an extreme twisting stretch to the forearms and that you will want to disengage your fingers. Sweet agony!

4 Hold the hands tight and try to straighten the elbows as far as possible. Hold this position for 30 seconds and then gently release.

5 Repeat three times.

6 Change sides, bringing the left hand over the right and repeat four times.

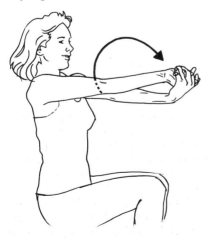

Chapter Ten

THE

WRISTS

WHAT IS THE WRIST?

The wrist to the hand is like the ankle to the foot. What goes on in the hand is decided by how well the wrist can position itself for the best activity of the fingers and thumb. You will have seen in the previous chapter on elbows that the forearm and the interplay of its two bones – the radius and the ulna – are also intimately involved in hand and fingers function. These two bones provide the larger-scale background positioning, setting the stage for the finer movements further down the arm. As one gets down to the fingertips, the precision of the function intensifies with the fine adjustments of hair's-breadth work superimposing themselves on the coarser ones, all the way back to the shoulder. The shoulder moves the whole arm about; the elbow varies the hand's distance from the body; the forearm decides on the attitude of the hand; and the wrist decides on the positioning of the thumb and fingers.

As far as the parallel with the lower limb goes, the attitude of the lower leg has an almost minimal role to play in the activity at the foot and toes. This is because the leg is largely a pillar of support, balance and ambulation. With very little variety in movements, it just keeps walking. In contrast, the arm is called upon to come up with an infinite variety of positions and movements, from the grandiose to the finicky.

The wrist proper is made up of eight small bones called the carpal bones. They are the mobile base for the fingers. Simply speaking, they arrange themselves in two rows between the bottom of the radius in the forearm and the metacarpal bones of the palm of the

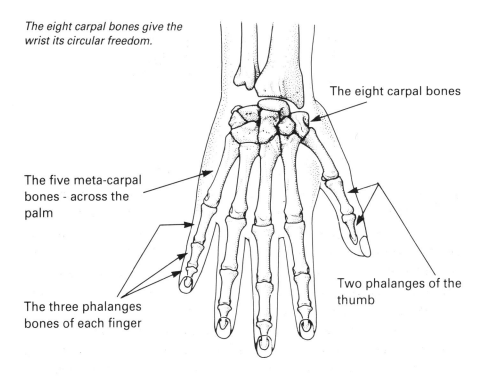

The eight carpal bones give the wrist its circular freedom.

The eight carpal bones

The five meta-carpal bones - across the palm

The three phalanges bones of each finger

Two phalanges of the thumb

hand. The metacarpal bones fan out from the front of the carpal block and join with the fingers at the knuckles. They are slender and delicate, their loosely held side-by-side harmony giving the palm its own degree of mobility. They allow the palm, with the help of the bases of the thumb and the little finger to have its own moulding type of grip, the background facilitator of precision thumbwork.

The carpal bones are situated at the base of the hand, just beyond the knob we see on the outside of the wrist, and they spread across the hand in a two-centimetre (almost one-inch) band before the metacarpals start. Only the bone on the upper side of the forearm (the radius) articulates with the block of the carpal bones. The other bone (the ulna) does not. It sits back, walled off from the carpal bones by a wedge of cartilage called the articular disc.

How Does the Wrist Work?

When the forearm goes about its function, the ulna stays still along the underside of the forearm and the radius rotates around it. The radius attaches through the carpal block to the hand. As it spins on its own axis it flaps the hand over with it; the forearm deciding the attitude of the hand – anywhere between palm up to palm down. The bottom of the ulna is not impinged upon at all by movement of the hand and the radius; the only movement that could bother it – a pure sideways movement of the hand in an outward direction – is cushioned by the presence of the articular disc of cartilage.

Then we come to the workings of the carpal bones. Working as a whole, they give the wrist that universal 360-degree freedom, superimposing another dimension of freedom on top of the 180 degrees of rotation of the forearm. They can move as a block or independently. Moving as a block, they alter the attitude of the hand's grasp, taking the fingers and the thumb through a conical range of freedom. Working as independent units within the block, they enhance the individual movement of the fingers. They do this in the following way. The eight carpal bones form two rows across the wrist, a front row and a back row. Roughly speaking they form up in blocks of two, one behind the other, each pair corresponding to one finger. (Having said that, the thumb and the index finger actually share three carpal bones between them.) Take the little finger, for example. Back up in the base of the hand, two carpal bones one behind the other contribute movement towards the metacarpal for that finger and thence on to the finger itself. This multiple source of fine movement gives the little finger a much greater depth of function than it would have if the finger simply sprouted from the end of the palm.

This is much more important to the thumb, since it is the superiority of this digit which makes us different from our nearest living forms of life, the apes. It is quite amazing how the thumb can move and the seemingly endless variety of things it allows the hand to do. In truth, most of the generosity of thumb movement comes from the junction of its metacarpal with its carpal bone rather than inter-carpal movement. But even so, inter-carpal freedom sets the stage as we shall see.

WHAT ARE THE ACCESSORY MOVEMENTS OF THE WRISTS?

The wrist is actually one big bag of bones, jam-packed full of accessory movement. The movement between all the carpal bones can best be described as synchronous. All of them shuffle and glide with movement in the same way as the bones of the tarsal block do in the foot. However, there is one carpal bone whose movement is rather different. This is the lunate. This bone sits in the middle of the back row, right under the eave of the overhanging shelf of the radius. It is thinner at the back of the hand than it is on the underside – the palmar side of the hand. This means that as it bobs up and down in harmony with the rest of the bones of the carpus, its wedge shape makes it freer to glide one way than the other.

HOW DOES THE WRIST GO WRONG?

If the hand is functioning normally the wrist suffers little in the way of wear and tear. However, if the wrists are subjected to inordinate amounts of pushing or are forced to bear weight with the palm flat they will give trouble; all because of the shape of the lunate.

If the hand is forced back, the carpal bone at the front of the lunate (the capitate) will angle up towards the shelf of the radius and in so doing, squeeze the lunate out. The degree of wedging of the lunate varies from individual to individual but broadly speaking the more forcibly the wrist is forced back, the more the lunate tends to ooze out at the front of the wrist.

This is particularly so if the pressure is exerted on the wrist at an angle; more through the outside heel of the hand rather than directly flat against the hand. The reasons for this are rather technical but worth explaining.

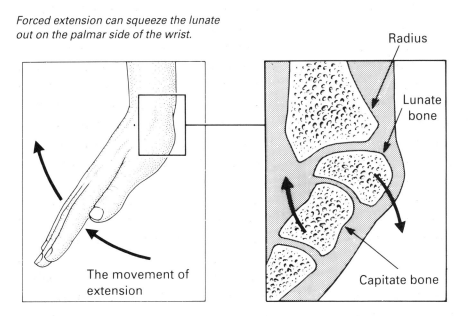

Forced extension can squeeze the lunate out on the palmar side of the wrist.

The movement of extension

Radius

Lunate bone

Capitate bone

108

There is another bone of the carpal block at the base of the thumb, called the scaphoid, which locks the wrist and prevents it from going any further back. It does this earlier in the range of the bending back movement than the lunate does. The scaphoid naturally blocks the wrist's backward movement by jamming itself between the radius and the trapezium – the carpal bone in front of it. For this lock to engage before the lunate does, the hand must be bent back evenly and not at an angle. If it does come back at an angle, with the heel of the hand before the thumb side of the hand, the lunate will be pinched out before the scaphoid lock can block the movement and prevent damage.

THE COMMON DISORDERS OF THE WRIST
The Sprained Wrist

The sprained wrist is the result of the above-mentioned process, usually caused by a fall on the outstretched hand. The heel of the hand comes down first and forces the wrist backwards and the lunate is forced out. There may be partial or complete rupture of the ligaments holding the lunate in position and even frank dislocation of the lunate out of its niche in the carpal block – a particularly unpleasant injury. But more importantly for the purposes of this book, trouble can also develop as a chronic degenerating condition if you do a lot of activity which involves taking weight through the flat of your hand. Many people come into this category – jack-hammer operators, bread makers, cyclists, acrobats. Even physiotherapists like me. There I am delving around in prostrate human spines all day, using the heel of my hand all the time to persuade some blocked vertebra to move.

Perhaps more common is a situation in which the above two scenarios combine: an initial injury which never quite heals and which you then keep on hurting. The initial injury is often a fall but it can happen in other ways too: hurriedly pushing a door open with the heel of your hand, especially if the door happens to be locked! Forcing a half-shut car door completely shut instead of opening it and slamming it again is a criminal thing to do to a wrist. You would be better taking your shoe off and kicking the door shut with your foot. But don't hurt the foot – or the door.

Like the ankle, the sheer number of small bones and multiple joints in the area makes sure that the stretching and tearing when you do your first wrench is not simply localised to one joint. Of course, it is always possible that the trauma is of sufficient force to break bone rather than tear soft tissue. In some respects this injury bodes better for the future of both joints – the ankle and the wrist – since the force taken up by snapping the bone at least spares the widespread wrenching of soft tissue. I think it is true to say too, that fractures are treated better than sprains by the medical profession. A short (I repeat 'short') spell in plaster of Paris often leaves a better joint than a badly sprained one, simply because the sprained ones are so often ignored. If you sprain it rather than break it you are often told to rest for a bit and not use the wrist (or ankle). You then gingerly start to use it in your own time – when really it needed movement from the start – graded movement under the care of a competent physiotherapist.

Having said that, a fracture of the scaphoid is not a welcome event. It has a particularly poor blood supply and often heals very slowly or not at all. If you fall on your outstretched hand you can pulverise the scaphoid between the trapezium and the radius or even break the radius itself (called a Colles fracture) which is very common in little old ladies whose bones have become brittle. But a bad sprain, once done, never really goes away unless you stretch it properly as it recuperates and get back all its accessory movement.

―――――――――――― *Repetitive Strain Injury* ――――――――――

There is one other disorder of the wrist which does not strictly fall into the category of degenerative joint conditions but since it is an ailment directly related to paucity of function I have chosen to include it here. The condition is repetitive strain injuries or RSI. This is a problem caused by overuse of the arm, particularly in circumstances where there is very little variety in the way it is used. People who work on production lines complain of the problem, as do secretaries and word-processor operators who spend hours in a day bent over a keyboard. The problem lies not only in the repetition of the same movement but also in the movement itself being so meagre. Take the modern keyboard for instance; you hardly need to expend any effort at all but the activity is continuous. There is a complete absence of flamboyance and romp to the movement. There is not even the benefit of the old-fashioned carriage return which although in itself repetitive did at least provide some respite from the typing action by punctuating the monotonous fine finger movement with a good old bash at the lever at the right-hand of the typewriter. Not nowadays. If you watch a modern word-processor operator at work she hardly moves. On closer scrutiny you see that her fingers are minutely crawling all over the keys. The operator sits poised over the machine and the better ones it seems are worse off than the novices. At least the novices are always stopping and back-spacing to correct their work, which breaks the tempo (I'll never get RSI), whereas the good ones sit for hours at their machines, head still and often quaintly tilted to one side to read the copy, and the only thing moving is their fingers. I always used to wonder why they looked so demure. Now I see why.

Trouble is not only caused by the lack of variety and lack of swing and gusto in the movement which I will go on to explain in a minute, but also by the fact that the shoulders and the shoulder girdle must hold the arms, most particularly the wrists, suspended above the level of the keyboard. This constitutes major long-term postural strain across the back of the neck and over the shoulders. Of course, good technique and properly considered relative chair and desk height make a big difference, helping eliminate the latter problem. But it is hard to come to terms with the first two.

The best angle for the wrist to do things is cocked back at twenty degrees. This puts the tinkling key-pinging muscles of the fingers on a slight stretch but it also means that one group of muscles on the back of the wrist is statically holding the wrist over a lengthy period, to keep the fingers poised for action. At the same time the muscles on the underside of the wrist are the ones controlling the key-tapping.

As we saw in the chapter on shoulders, there are two different muscle types – the postural and phasic – which act in different ways. To recap briefly, all the postural muscles are found on the torso where they work to keep the skeleton upright. These are the muscles of the spine, the shoulder blade and the hips. Their efforts keep us from collapsing in a heap. As they have to work all the time, their contraction is low in intensity to economise on energy consumption. Their muscle fibres are different too, reflecting this different function. The other group is the phasic muscles, or the 'doers'. As I said earlier, these are the muscles you decide to use if you are swatting a fly or conducting a symphony orchestra. They only work when required and have long periods when they don't need to act; not many flies about. The point is that phasic muscles cannot take on the role of postural muscles. In the case of the wrist, it severely taxes the muscles of the wrists and fingers if they are asked to keep the wrist propped back, and still, while the fingers do their thing. Fatigue is the first problem and inflammation the next.

There are eleven tendons which operate across the palmar side of the wrist and twelve across the back. They travel in their own tube of fibrous tissue called a tendon sheath which minimises friction of one working tendon against its neighbours and also lubricates the tendon. The tendons all pass under a fibrous band at the wrist called the retinaculum. This is like a watch strap front and back, and it keeps the tendons contained. It also prevents them webbing up the skin of the wrist as they contract and thus keeps the tension on each tendon while it does what it has to do in the hand.

You can see without any exaggeration that this is a tight fit; all those tendons bunched in cheek by jowl as they work. If you also add to this the fact that tendons unlike muscles do not have a drenching blood supply and must rely on lubrication by their tendon sheath, then you have a recipe for trouble if their work is arduous. No – arduous is not the word. I mean if their work is minimal in effort, and long-term. Arduous would be a good thing; then at least the muscles and their tendons would have the benefit of powerful muscle contractions with their massive suction effect on the circulation, pulling in swamping supplies of blood to feed the muscle contraction. As it is with the word-processor operator, there isn't much of that. Also there is very little stretch-and-release of the muscle and tendon tissue as it acts; the keyboarding movement is too small. The stretch would help yield a higher blood supply to the working tissue. But there is none of that. There is only tiny finger movements, each tendon doing its own little puppet string-pulling to give an almost imperceptible dab at the fingertips on the keypads.

The close proximity of all the tendons in the wrist is also a problem, especially since tendon tissue is so relatively bloodless. With repetitive meagre action, there is real cause for overheating.

Poor lubrication, a direct result of inadequate blood supply for the reasons outlined above, causes friction of tendon against tendon sheath. Inflammation is the result. The pain can be excruciating. Whenever that particular tendon is active there will be a nasty prick of pain. If severe, there will be a glancing, shooting sear of pain, so intense that you can't go on. The wrist or the tendon running back up the arm can be hot to the touch. This is RSI – inflammation of the tendon and the tendon sheath.

The solution in the early stages is ice and rest. Only rest for a matter of days though, before you start the stretching exercises. To prevent this condition from developing in the first place you need to maintain generosity in variety of movement. If only all employers did what the South Koreans do with their factory workers: have regular callisthenic exercise sessions to open out the skeleton and drench the musculature with a soaking blood supply. But until that happens, start yourself on the following stretch regime.

WHAT CAN YOU DO ABOUT IT?

Quite dramatic loosening of the composite carpal block can be achieved simply by stretching the long finger flexor muscles of the forearm. These are the fleshy bulk on the inside of the forearm, whose tendons span the front of the wrist and go through to curl the fingers.

The following stretches loosen the tension of the bow-string action of these muscles and unjam the carpal bones, optimising their individual freedom.

E X E R C I S E   1

The Interlaced Finger Stretch

You will need a chair for this exercise.

1 Sit squarely on the chair with your feet on the floor, the back held straight and the fingers firmly laced together in your lap.

2 Raise your arms above your head, pushing your interlaced palms towards the ceiling. Keep your elbows straight and your upper arms level with or behind your ears (from the side view your arms will make a continuous line with your body).

3 Hold the position for 1 minute. You will be surprised how difficult it is but don't trap your breath – breathe deeply and regularly. Your fingers will try to disengage but keep them tightly locked and then bring them down gently, back to your lap.

4 Repeat three times.

5 Now disengage your fingers and

reclasp them in the next web along and repeat the exercise four times.

E X E R C I S E   2

The Kneeling Rock

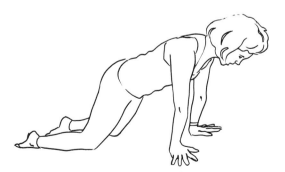

1 Start on your hands and knees on the floor, palms down but your fingers turned out to an angle of approximately thirty degrees.

2 Rock forwards on your knees so your weight comes over your hands and on to your wrists, especially the inner side of the wrists.

3 Rock backwards and forwards several times. Each time attempt to go a little further forwards.

EXERCISE 3

The Reverse Prayer

You will need a chair for this exercise.

1 Sit squarely on the chair with your feet firmly on the floor and your back held up straight.

2 Turning both arms inwards at the shoulder, take first your left hand and then your right hand up behind your back. Bring the tips of your hands together and then the rest of your hands, to put the hands in a prayer position behind your back. Keep the heels of the hands pressed firmly together.

3 Hold the position for 60 seconds then release.

4 Repeat once.

115

Chapter Eleven

THE HIPS

WHAT IS THE HIP?

The hip joints are two deeply set ball-and-socket joints which are the articulation between the top of the legs and the bottom of the torso. The round tennis-ball-shaped head of the thigh bone or femur buries itself deep into a cup-shaped socket, the acetabulum, in either side of the pelvis and forms a modestly generous universal joint. While we are standing, the cup and the head are aligned in such a way that although they are the same size the cup does not quite cover the head of the femur. This can only be brought about if the upper leg assumes the position of kneeling – as one does on all fours – which adds credence to the theory that we are descended from a form which crawled rather than walked.

The head of the femur is covered with thick densely spongy glistening cartilage which absorbs shock and aids friction-free movement of the ball in the socket. It is thickest at the top of the cavity and at the top of the head where the full weight of the body bears down upon it. The head is kept in place in the socket by the presence of a capsule, a tubular sleeve of rather inelastic but strong tissue which extends from the rim of the acetabulum to the base of the neck of the femur, wrapping the two components of the joint together. The capsule is reinforced by denser bands of tissue all around, the ligaments, which further adds stability to the joint.

The hip joint. The internal struts of bone, or trabeculae, provide internal shoring to bolster the strength where the bone is most subject to stress.

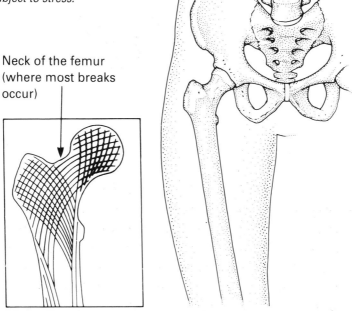

Neck of the femur
(where most breaks
occur)

The long shaft of the femur has its job of approach and access into either side of the pelvis made easier by the design of the neck of the femur. This forms an angle of roughly 125 degrees with the shaft, an ideal angle for dispersing the weight coming down from the femoral head through a diagonal strut across to the vertical shaft. It has even been shown on examples of dried human bone that there are multiple fine struts of internal bone – the trabeculae – which directly follow the lines of force here in the upper end of the femur. The trabeculae exist in places where the bone is most subject to stress. But what is particularly fascinating is that the confluence of these struts takes the form of a Gothic arch. At the point of intersection of these myriad fine pillars of internal bone – their keystones – the overall density of the bone is much greater and therefore more able to withstand stress. These points correspond exactly to where the bone needs the most help: the centre of the head of the femur, to withstand crushing; and the base of the neck of the femur, to withstand shear. So here we have the beauty of Nature repeating itself! Gothic arches all over the place, not only in the finest cathedrals in the land but all through our own bones. It is also interesting to note that the parts in the head-neck-shaft arrangement of the femur which don't have this internal reinforcement are exactly where the hip is weakest and where the bone is most likely to break. This is exactly what happens as the bones become frailer in old age – as little old ladies fall over in the street and fracture the necks of their femurs. The bone is the weakest where the neck joins the shaft and when it breaks it breaks here – a shearing break, right through the neck of the femur. Surgical pinning is the answer, where a shaft of metal is driven up through the neck to prop the head and neck up again in correct weight-bearing alignment.

118

How Do the Hips Work?

It could be said that the hips sacrifice mobility for stability, their chief functions being ones of balanced standing and locomotion. They are sensationally strong joints and to a degree this is their nemesis. There is no other joint of the skeleton more trapped by habit.

For the most part, the hips simply angle back and forwards as they do during walking. The equality of length of stride is the all-important factor in joint health. Any discrepancy has far-reaching manifestations, most notably pain. All manner of aches and pains throughout the body: hip pain, chronic low back pain, chest pain or even migraine headaches can be caused by the unequal twisting action induced on the human skeleton during walking. Length of stride is directly dependent on the freedom of the backward direction at the hip, called extension. This is perhaps the least generous movement at the hip and any loss of movement here will be more noticeable than a similar loss of movement in the forwards direction,

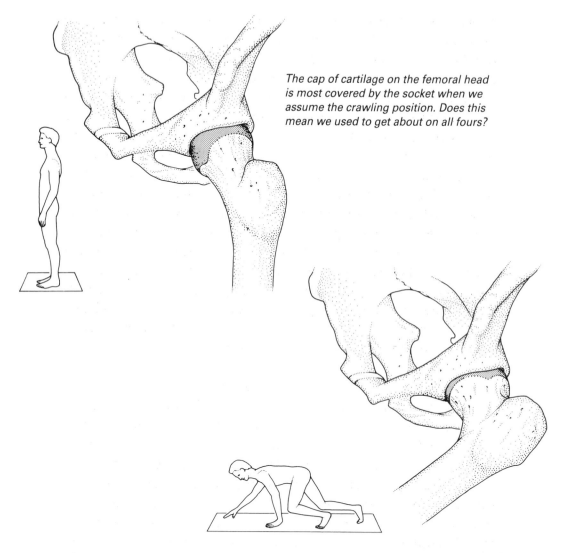

The cap of cartilage on the femoral head is most covered by the socket when we assume the crawling position. Does this mean we used to get about on all fours?

flexion. The hip angles back only about twenty degrees but it bends the other way, thigh on to chest about 130 degrees. Easy to see, therefore, that a deficit of fifteen degrees in flexion will have very little consequence whereas a loss of fifteen degrees of extension will be almost everything. Sadly, it is not that difficult to lose extension and its freedom can be clipped by other specific factors, most notably where one leg is longer than the other.

The hip of the longer leg loses extension because when standing, its extra length makes it adopt a slight bend at the hip and at the knee. It does this to compensate for its extra length, to make it possible for the pelvis to sit straight and ultimately for our eyes to be level at the top of the vertebral column. Over time, this bend becomes irreversible and is known as a contracture of the hip (and knee). With every step there is a twist of the spine as the skeleton compensates for inability of the hip of the longer leg to go into extension. This also means that the length of stride taken on the shorter leg is reduced. The discrepancy profoundly alters our whole pattern of gait. Does it matter, you might ask? Well, just think about the number of steps we take. Is it 10,000 a day? At that number, it surely does matter.

Incidentally while on the subject of reduced hip extension, women universally have less extension than men. This is brought about by a tightness of the ilio-femoral ligament which runs down across the front of the hip joint. It is of no momentous significance but it accounts for the typically feminine mincing gait and waggling bottom, so common in women and not usually men.

What are the Accessory Movements of the Hips?

The hip is such a deeply-set joint that it has a minimum of the more subtle variety of accessory movements like glide and shuffle. The one of most importance to the hip is distraction. This is the movement where there is some slipping out or separation of the ball from the socket; where the head of the femur is distracted from its cup within the pelvis.

As discussed above, the forces sustained by the round hemi-spherical heads of femurs are immense; all the weight of the body bears down on a relatively small area over the upper crest of each head. These forces are profoundly intensified during the acts of running and jumping so that whatever the activity, the maintenance of the health of the head of the femur is of critical importance. As it happens, the blood supply to the head and neck of the femur cannot be described as abundant. As a further drawback, that blood supply finds access to the hip joint via arterial branches which pass through the actual capsule of the hip. One small extra artery comes via a small ligament which attaches directly on to the head of the femur – the ligamentum teres. This ligament originates in the floor of the socket and attaches just below the top of the dome of the hemi-spherical head and it performs an ancillary role of keeping the head of the femur in the socket.

It is slightly less than ideal to have the vessels supplying blood to the hip so intimately involved with the ligamentous and capsular tissue of the hip, since the health of this tissue can be the health of the blood supply. For example, if the capsule were to develop the typically thickened dry and inelastic quality of a lazy stiff joint, very common for hips, the ambience of easy passage for the arterial vessels will be threatened. A certain elastic quality to the hip will do the opposite. It will enhance the flow of blood through the joint. It works like this. As you walk you transfer your weight from one leg to the other. When you shift your weight off your leg, the weight of the leg drags the head of the femur out of the socket and the blood vessels are attenuated. As the body weight comes back on to that leg again and the head slides back up into the socket, there will be a simultaneous elastic recoil of the vessels and tissues which have been on the stretch. As you walk, a harmonious pumping rhythm is set up which greatly enhances the routine blood flow through the joint, particularly important in this joint which has a poor blood supply.

How Do Hips Go Wrong?

As a race, we Westerners use our hips appallingly. We restrict them to a rigidly stereotyped pattern of use. All we do is walk on them; an excursion of movement which takes them through a very limited arc of movement. Then we sit for a bit, or a lot, and this very act of sitting merely arrests the hips at some fixed point in the arc through which they move when we walk. At the end of the day we lie down and they go straight, a position rather like standing, but at least they bear no weight. As you can see, there is not much in the way of variety through their daily toil. Every now and then we may break the monotony and take a giant step up on to a chair to get the biscuit barrel from the top of the cupboard, or take a step sideways on the pavement to avoid a puddle but not often. For the most part we use our hips with a monotonous lack of imagination. I mean, how long is it since you saw an adult hang upside down from a gate? We hardly ever do things like that. We just grind them back and forth over that same limited territory, gouging a narrow track in the cartilage and ignoring all the other possibilities. We never use them as I see my son doing now, for example; climbing a tree, one knee up under the chin and the toes of the other foot straining to get push-off from some bough way below, almost out of reach.

Oriental races who have a penchant for sitting cross-legged on the floor rarely develop hip disease. It appears that their hips benefit from the variety and extremes of positioning; knees akimbo and the hips unweighted, widely separated in an unfunctional pose. Here, unlike the conventional Western sitting posture, the hips experience a freedom which for any other purpose is useless – useless but essential for health.

THE COMMON DISORDERS OF THE HIPS
Arthritis

Osteoarthritis is the commonest affliction of the hip. It is the premature ageing of a joint where ordinary wear and tear has been intensified by outside forces acting upon the hip. These may be subtle factors such as the discrepancy of leg length mentioned above, where asymmetry of the skeleton takes its toll over time; or may be the result of much more flamboyant trauma of a one-off variety such as a previous break to the bone or freak dislocation of the joint. In this instance, the past shake-up to the joint will have done some lasting damage. In the case of a fracture, faulty union may have left the bones in poor alignment but whatever the trauma when the hip has been injured there will be a legacy of dysfunction which goes on to fuel further chronic breakdown. The hip's relatively poor blood supply and its limited range of movement make it more susceptible than most to self-destruction. The wear and tear on these joints is enormous. Two factors play big roles in thwarting this breakdown: cartilage, and synovial fluid.

Hyaline cartilage is the smooth pearly stuff that moulds itself to ends of bone, interposing itself in a cushioning way between the rigid bone of the ball and the socket. In the human hip it is very thick, especially over the head of the femur, and as such is an excellent shock absorber. The smooth slipperiness of the surface of cartilage also helps disperse shock. As your heel strikes the ground each time you take a step (that incessant heel strike – what was it, 10,000 steps a day?) the cartilage is hard to compress and yet it does yield. This miraculous unwilling compliance of cartilage adds another dimension to the quality of human movement. With a flexibility rather like that of the dense plastic of a plastic washing-up bowl, cartilage sinks and springs with every movement. We advance with that miraculous glide; we lope rather than totter, and we spare the juddering of our bones.

In short the glossier, the thicker, and the springier the cartilage, the better. This is no small order, considering the wear and tear it suffers. Nourishment and maintenance of the cartilage is a key issue in the human hip. But cartilage does not have its own blood supply and this is where the second factor comes in – lubricating fluid called synovial fluid.

Each large joint of the skeleton is encapsulated in a bag of lubricating fluid. It has three simple functions: it acts as fluid dampener or hydraulic sac, cushioning the shock between the two bones; it feeds the cartilage and thereby keeps it alive; and it filters itself, dissolving fragments of cartilage debris floating in its midst. It does this by means of large cartilage-eating cells which devour any fragments of floating cartilage chipped off during the wear and tear of movement. So, by keeping itself immersed in and thoroughly awash with this synovial fluid the cartilage is prevented from scouring, chafing, splitting, chipping and drying out. This is where the freedom of the joint again comes in.

Getting the synovial fluid right through the full thickness of the cartilage is a feat. Of course, it is the superficial layers of cartilage which bear the brunt of the chipping and grinding action of two bones working on each other but these layers are in immediate contact with the synovial fluid and can easily have their troubled toil soothed. The deeper layers also need to be reached. Their nourishment relies solely on a press-release effect of alternating pressure within the joint. Rather like forcing water through a dense sponge, the alternating pressures of active movement drive fresh fluids into the deeper layers of cartilage and suck old fluids out, keeping the whole cartilage healthy and young.

The more dramatic the change in pressure generated within the joint, the more efficient this shunting and sucking pump mechanism is. A looser joint makes a better pump. The looser the joint, the more the bones of the joint can move apart in the non-weight-bearing phase of its activity and the greater the drag effect of the fluid out of the tissues. And then during the bone-contact phase, the further apart from which the two bones come together, the greater the change in pressure generated within the joint. You can see here I'm sure, another example of the value of accessory movement; a movement which may defy the most myopic scrutiny but which is there nevertheless.

There is another equally important way in which the joints are the beneficiaries of generous joint mobility: stimulation of synovial fluid. The synovial fluid is secreted by the synovial membrane which lines the inner wall of the joint capsule. In rather the same way that tears flush the eyes and mucus the nasal cavities, synovial fluid pours into the joint space and keeps the lubrication going. The genius factor here is that the more the joint capsule is tugged and pulled by flamboyant movement, the more synovial fluid is released. Where the movements are meagre, repetitive and generally undemanding, the secretion of synovial lubrication remains at a modicum; just adequate to keep the bones afloat, but nothing to write home about. In contrast, where the movement is vigorous stretching and generally very taxing, the response by the joint is totally different. There is a massive flushing through the joint, a beautiful dynamic exchange of fluid in and out of the joint so that the joint is kept healthy; clean fluid keeping its surfaces young.

If you have arthritis, this does not happen and the cartilage is the first to suffer. Although all our joints get drier as we get older, this process is speeded up with arthritis. An arthritic hip usually comes on insidiously. The first sign will be a vague tightness of the hip on certain movements. This is frequently passed off as 'just a stiff hip' but you will be increasingly troubled by it. You may not notice your gait changing yet but you will find it difficult to do some actions: getting down to tie your shoelaces; and almost as much lifting the foot up on to a chair. Putting tights or socks on is also a trial and in severe cases you may have to resort to using a ruler or some other long apparatus to pull the clothing over your foot. In really bad cases, you may have to bend your foot up behind you, grab the sock and then pull it up your leg. All time-consuming and awkward stuff, not to mention painful. The pain usually appears after the stiffness although, of course, there are exceptions to that rule and pain may be the first to appear. If so it is usually felt deep in the groin as a gnawing discomfort, made worse by walking, but sometimes worse in bed at night. It may also be felt over the outer side of the hip and possibly in a referred band down the front of the thigh to the knee. There are no hard and fast rules; there are instances of crippling arthritic changes seen on X-ray films, where you have no hip discomfort, only a referred pain in the knee; just as there are instances of crippling arthritic changes in the hip and not one skerrick of pain felt anywhere.

In the early stages X-ray pictures can be confusing, precisely because they show so little. Usually at the beginning, discomfort is the only sign followed by tangible loss of movement. With hips, perhaps more than any other joint, the early findings on X-rays appear to conflict with what the patient says. Not so in advanced cases, where the films will show a marked reduction in the joint space caused by thinning of the cartilage, and knobbly outgrowths of excess bone at the margins of the joint – osteophytes.

In extremes, the head of the femur will no longer have its rounded tennis-ball shape but will be flattened and irregular, a great impediment to streamlined performance. This flattening also causes shortening of the affected leg which leads to the characteristic rolling sailor's gait.

Like all joints, there is an idiosyncratic pattern in the way the joint loses mobility. The first movement to wane is the backwards movement of the leg at the hip (extension). The next is the movement of taking the leg out sideways from the other leg (abduction), and also inward rotation of the hip, the turning in of the foot. The walking gait exhibits a lack of all these movements: the foot turned out and one leg in close to the other leg, sometimes crossing in front of it and giving a scissors gait. And because this leg cannot angle backwards at the hip, the length of stride forwards on the good leg must be reduced in length with the whole body having to twist to compensate. If the head of the femur has flattened and the leg has shortened, you will stand with your weight resting only on the toes of the foot and when walking you will have the sailor's lurching action as you drop down on to the shorter leg.

WHAT CAN YOU DO ABOUT IT?

What do you need? Generous movement, movement and more movement; even if your hip is bad. Keep the variety up, keep high-impact activities down. By keeping the avenues of non-functional movement open, the quality of everyday movement is enhanced. Keep the joints juicy and slack enough to sluice wave after wave of fresh cleansing blood through, and guarantee the joints' maintenance. Keep the joints loose enough so that the head of the femur can move about and does not gouge a single track in the cartilage of the acetabulum; the forces are distributed more widely across a greater surface area. Perpetuate 'looseness'.

Early attention to stretching exercises, especially if you are involved in activities such as running and tennis, will thwart the development of arthritic hip disease which is devastatingly painful

126

and disruptive to a normal active life. Even though arthritic hip disease is common enough to make surgical hip replacements the most often performed orthopaedic procedure, following a modest regime of these yoga stretches will defy the day.

EXERCISE 1

The Buttock Stretch

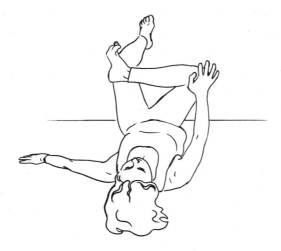

Find a clear wall with some uncluttered space in front of it.

1 Lie on your back on the floor with your bottom far enough away from the wall so that by resting your left foot on the wall, your hip and knee bend by ninety degrees each.

2 Bring your right foot up and place its outside ankle on top of your left knee.

3 Applying gentle pressure with your right hand, push the right knee away from you towards the wall. Bounce it gently for 2 minutes trying to push it a little further with each bounce.

4 Take your left foot down from the wall and change sides. Repeat once for each side.

5 With practice you will be able to progress the exercise and either point the toe on the wall or bring your bottom closer to the wall for a greater stretch at the hip.

EXERCISE 2

The Knees Apart Stretch

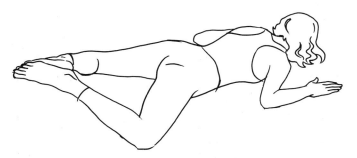

1 Kneel on your hands and knees on the floor with your knees as far apart as they will go while keeping your big toes pressed together.
2 Lower yourself forwards on to your hands, pivoting on your knees, and lay the front of your chest down on the floor. Your bottom will remain perched up in the air and your feet will come up. The stiffer your hips, the higher your bottom will be off the floor.
3 Stay there for 1 minute, allowing your knees to creep further apart as your hips release. This will lower your bottom.
4 Push yourself back with your hands and sit back on your heels and rest.
5 Repeat three times.

EXERCISE 3

The Dead Blow Fly

1 Lie on your back on the floor and bring both knees up to your chest and out closer to your armpits.
2 Raise your feet so your knees make a right-angle and the soles of your feet face the ceiling.
3 Grab the outer side of both feet with your hands and pull the knees closer to your armpits.
4 Hold the position for 30 seconds and release.
5 Repeat three times.

EXERCISE 4

The Up-and-Down Hip Stretch

You will need a kitchen chair for this.
1 Kneel on the floor in front of the chair.
2 Grasp the back of the chair to keep stable and keeping your left knee on the floor lift your right foot up on to the chairseat. If this is too difficult, start from the opposite direction: stand in front of the chair, lift your right foot on to the seat, then sink down on to your left knee on the floor. Whichever way you approach this, don't let your hips kink and your bottom poke out and try to keep your back straight. If both these methods are too difficult you may need to start with a lower chair or to place a thick telephone directory under your knee.
3 Hold the position for 1 minute and release.
4 Repeat with the other leg.

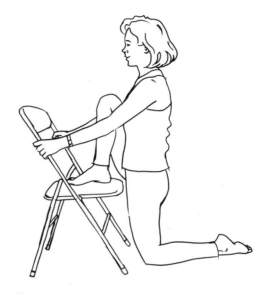

5 Repeat the sequence two more times for each leg.

EXERCISE 5

The Floor Lunge

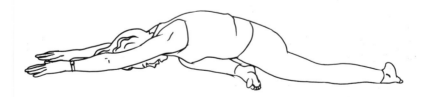

1 Kneel on the floor on all fours. Bring your right leg up and bring the foot through in front of the left knee so that it rests on the floor in front of the left groin.

2 Straighten the left leg at the knee and the hip by moving it backwards along the floor and sink your body down on to the right foot trapped under the left groin.

3 Try to keep your body low and straight along the floor and resist the temptation for the body to roll to the right, off the trapped leg.

4 Maintain the position for 30 seconds and then lift your weight back with your hands.

5 Repeat once and change sides and repeat twice.

6 With practice you can progress this exercise by moving the foot of the trapped leg up in an arc away from the groin and lying down on it again. Maximum freedom of the hip allows the lower leg to lie transversely across the floor under your belly. Very few people have this much freedom and invariably it is easier to do one side than the other.

Chapter Twelve

THE

KNEES

What is the Knee?

The knee joint allows us to bend the leg. Like the elbow, it resembles a simple hinge. It is formed by the junction with the bottom of the thigh-bone – the femur – and the top of the shin-bone – the tibia. The smaller bone on the outer side of the lower leg – the fibula – is not involved in the joint and simply serves as bony attachment for some of the muscles which work the foot. As such, the fibula does not help in the load of bearing weight. In fact the elephant is the only living creature which bears weight through its fibulae. All the rest of us bear weight only through our tibiae.

The kneecap or patella is a shield-shaped device covered in smooth cartilage which floats in front of the knee joint. It is embedded in the tendon of the high muscles, the quadriceps, which run down across the front of the knee joint and attach into the bump that we kneel on at the top of the tibia. The role of the patella is to defray the friction of the quadriceps tendon pulling and releasing as the knee bends and straightens. The quadriceps muscle shortens as it contracts and so pulls the tendon around the angle of the knee, in

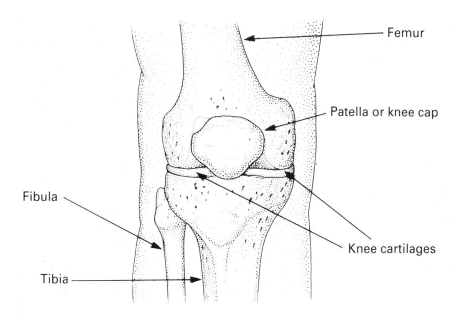

Femur

Patella or knee cap

Fibula

Knee cartilages

Tibia

The right knee joint: the miraculous locking hinge.

rather the same fashion that a woman pulls up her stockings over her knee. This action has the effect of pulling the lower leg and the foot forwards and straightening the leg. But like rope, the tendon would fray with the continual pulley-like action of the tendon working around the corner of the bent knee. The skidding, glistening cartilage of the patella stops all that.

The way the shape of the lower end of the femur works with the tibia gives some clue to how the hinge works to allow such an astonishing range of bend at the knee. The bottom end of the femur is rounded into two distinct lumps and so resembles two wheels. These are called the femoral condyles. Broadly speaking, the weight-bearing surface of the tibia is scooped into a saucer so that it fits snugly against the rounded condyles of the femur. As the knee bends, the wheel-shaped condyles roll backwards over the surface of the tibia while at the same time the tibia slides to the back of the condyles. So, not only does the wheel move over the ground but the ground also moves under the wheel; the movement of the lower bone ensuring the femur does not drive off the back of the tibia; and twice as much distance is covered rather like pulling a carpet away as wheels drive over it, there is a combination of both spin and glide, one bone moving in relation to the other. This results in a much greater movement and much greater range of bend of the knee.

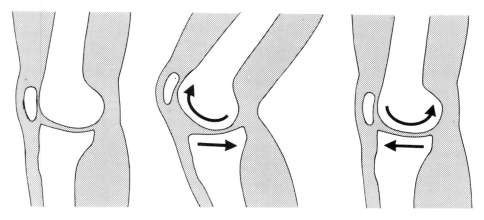

As we bend the knee, the femoral condyles roll back over the tibial plateau as the tibia itself glides back too. As we straighten, the condyles drive forwards, and the tibia glides forwards. Very efficient!

As the leg straightens the opposite happens; the femur drives forwards and then as the tibia comes more in line with the femur it glides forwards to line up with the femur, thus making sure it keeps under the wheels. With the two bones doing their bit, in no time at all the leg is straight. Such a clever arrangement, if you think about it. It not only gives the knee a fabulous range with minimum effort when bending but, from a simplistic point of view, it does away with the yawning V-shaped divot which would otherwise open up at the front of a bending knee if it worked like a simple hinge.

The knee is held together by ligaments at either side of the joint and by two ligaments which pass from the under surface of the femur to the top surface of the tibia. They twine through each other as they go, making a cross, and for this reason they are called the cruciate ligaments. Their role is to prevent the top bone slipping off the bottom one.

Two crescent-shaped scoops of cartilage, the menisci, on the weight-bearing surface of the tibia, further stabilise the action of the knee. As the knee bends and straightens and the wheels of the femoral condyles travel back and forwards over the tibia, their passage is kept in check by the cartilages of the knee. Seen in cross-section these are wedge-shaped, which pads out the gap between the round wheel-like base of the femur and the flat table-like surface of the tibia. Like railway tracks, the menisci dampen the potential wobble as one bone moves in relation to the other.

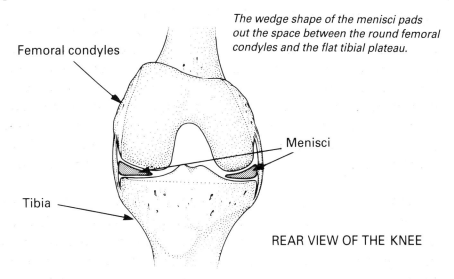

The wedge shape of the menisci pads out the space between the round femoral condyles and the flat tibial plateau.

Femoral condyles

Menisci

Tibia

REAR VIEW OF THE KNEE

How Does the Knee Work?

When the knee bends fully it can go from straight to about 140 degrees, so that your heel hits your bottom. During the act of walking it only bends through approximately 20 degrees. The way it 'locks' when the knee is almost straight is brought about by several factors: the fall of the terrain of the lower bony surface; the fact that the inner wheel or condyle of the femur is smaller that the outer one; the length and tautness of some of the controlling ligaments; and the pull of certain muscles which twist the femur in an inwards direction. They all act in concert to guide the upper leg 'home'. As the leg approaches full straightening, there is an inwards rotatory swivel of the upper leg on the lower one – almost like a screw-in mechanism. You can observe this in your own leg. Look down as you stand with your leg slightly bent at your knee. Brace the knee back straight, without moving your foot on the floor, and you will see an inward swivelling clonk of the thigh as your knee pushes back through its final degrees. This is locking, and swivelling is the action which does it.

So, if you thought that the knee was one joint which bends and straightens in one plane only you were wrong. What's more, this rotation element is vital to ongoing knee performance. The rotational accessory movement of the knee is even more critical than it is at other joints. A slacker joint like a shoulder, for example, can cope with a greater relative loss of accessory movement before dysfunction starts to show. This is because it has so many varieties of movement in its repertoire that it can find ways round problems or losses of accessory freedom. In a tighter joint such as the knee, a joint with a more singular purpose, this latitude does not exist. Even the slightest loss of joint 'play' will handicap its one important role.

WHAT ARE THE ACCESSORY MOVEMENTS OF THE KNEE?

The automatic locking mechanism of the knee is critical. It overcomes the problems of the dual roles of the leg; those of bendability and support. The locking mechanism allows us to brace the knee back and relax when taking weight on the straight leg. Without it we would consume vast amounts of energy simply in keeping our legs from buckling under us. The subtlety and fluency of this locking is even more spectacular during the highly complex act of walking. Here, as each leg passes from the support phase and on to the swing-through phase, the knee deftly locks and unlocks as weight passes on and off the leg. No volitional control at all. Just . . . sort of natural.

Forget about imagined miracles of walking on water and walking on air. The miracle is plain walking. The knee is a sensational joint.

For it to be as competent as it is – so strong and yet so lissom and compact – is truly amazing. So long and graceful, and yet it takes us from squatting on our haunches to standing in one lithe movement. It doesn't need pulleys and counter-balances and locking pins; just that slender coating of muscles . . . don't you think that's wonderful? The downside is that if it goes wrong, the knee is not a simple joint to replace artificially. Unlike the hip, where surgical replacements are quite easy, knee replacements are not such a breeze. The technology has only recently been more successful, simply because the manmade devices are so comparatively clumsy. Clever as we humans are, we are unable to create anything like the perfection that we find in nature.

How Do Knees Go Wrong?

With the knee, any deficit of accessory rotation will immediately impair the efficiency of the locking mechanism. Stability is the first casualty, in terms of lateral wobble when the knee is taking weight. Over time, this has a devastating effect on the cartilages of the knee. They soon show signs of wearing out. They become bruised and chipped; increasingly so the more the knee falls short of full straightening. More importantly, failure to gain complete lock of the knee means that the knee retains a small degree of permanent bend when you are standing. This invites other trouble, this time with the patella. With the working hinge of the knee coming up closer behind the patella during a resting stance (when the knee should be straight), abrasion is caused. The patella and the hinge are too close for comfort and as a result low-grade, ongoing friction is set up. The underside of the kneecap becomes scraped irritated and eventually inflamed. So you can see that inability to reach the full lock is positively bad for a knee. It is the main cause of all of the degenerating conditions of the knee.

THE COMMON DISORDERS OF THE KNEES
— *Degeneration of the Knee Cartilages* —

If the screw-home mechanism fails to lock, the knee will show an imperceptible lateral wobble when it takes weight. The knee cartilages are the first to take the brunt of the excess lateral movement, since their role is that of wedging the wheel-like condyles into a specific tracking domain on the top surface of the tibia. They are sorely tried by condyles which are constantly wobbling and slewing against the cartilage wedge when they are meant to be locked down. Splitting, tearing and chipping of the knee cartilages is only too possible and this accounts for the high incidence of cartilage trouble in the adolescent to ageing population, especially in those who play sports. The cartilages are exposed to all manner of abuse, with tags of cartilage pulling off the main meniscus and 'bucket-handle' tears (following the circular line of the cartilage) as examples of some of the more spectacular. In short, the cartilages are pulverised by femoral condyles which never reach the safety of 'home'; never quietly nestled in at full lock. As the cartilages become more eroded by the knee at near-lock, they become less competent at controlling the knee both during movement and when still. The situation deteriorates from a lateral wobble as the knee stands straight to wobbling also as the knee bends. The knee starts to track badly, 'bumping against the rails', as it bends and straightens. Then, the femoral wheels resemble a steamroller on the loose; the hard bony condyles pounding the daylights out of the buffering cartilages as the knee goes back and forth.

Knees which exhibit signs of cartilage trouble are the bane of the sportsman's life. These are the knees which click and grind during movement and which show a marked tendency to lock and give way on unguarded movement. The knee will often be painful and swell after strenuous activity, even when there has been no specific wrench. The condition deteriorates further once the muscle power to lock the knee has gone. This muscle, called the vastus medialis, lies on the inner side of the thigh and can be seen as a soft mounded contour just above the inside of the knee. Its specific function is to take the knee through its last fifteen degrees of straightening and to get it locked in home. If the knee joint has lost the ability to get straight because it is too tight, this muscle group, sensing that it has no role, quickly wastes away. In clinical practice you see this in nearly all problem knees, no matter what the original trouble was – patella, cartilages or old-fashioned arthritis – you find a skinny concave thigh above the knee and a muscle bulk of circumference much smaller than that of the good leg.

In the past, treatment was often aimed at the effect (that is muscle weakness of the vastus medialis) rather than the cause (lack of full straightening). Sportsmen would toil away for hours, lifting sandbags with their foot, trying to build up the bulk of the quadriceps muscle. Sadly, they should have been directing their energies to restoring the accessory function of the knee so that it would straighten and then, and only then, doing exercises to strengthen the muscle.

Today the operative procedures are a marked improvement on what they were even a few years ago. The realm of fibre optics has helped a great deal in reducing the violation of knees. Arthroscopies are a relatively simple procedure. Through a tiny incision, doctors insert a probe like a periscope into a knee and actually view the state of the cartilages. If surgical intervention is warranted it is but a simple job to do it through the same minute incision, using the same gadget. Gone are the days of the ten-centimetre (four-inch) scar and long post-operative periods taken up with lifting sandbags. What trembling physiotherapy student will forget the orthopaedic wards full of swaggering young bloods, all with vast pressure bandages around their knees, all of whom had to be massaged and cajoled into lifting their leg off the bed before they could be discharged from hospital?

Arthritis of the Knee

Cartilages are the first line of defence but actual trauma to the bony joint surfaces is not far behind. But beware! This is the beginning of arthritis of the knee; that awful term we hear so much about and associate with wheelchairs and forlorn images of debility.

Arthritis is the end result of years of excessive wear and tear on a knee. It exhibits all the hallmarks of a serious problem joint, pain being the salient factor. It hurts all the time; even lying in bed, when the knee has to be cradled on a pillow and even then can cause hours of interrupted sleep. Usually it is most tender along the inside joint line but the whole knee can be locked in the vice of a permanent humming ache. As it deteriorates, it quickly loses that fabulous streamlined quality of a healthy joint and becomes bloated by swelling and general thickening of its surrounding tissues. All movements become restricted; it will not straighten and will barely bend beyond ninety degrees. In advanced cases, the skin over the knee has an unhealthy pallor and also develops a shiny, papery quality. In addition, the knee will often feel hot to the touch, indicating the degree of inflammation going on underneath. Movement is often associated with disconcerting grating and rustling noises within the joint, called crepitus. Crepitus is an indication that the lubrication to the knee is below par and can be likened to a squeak in a wheel. Elderly people have to use a stick to get about and eventually a walking frame.

In the earlier stages, the knee goes through a dry, poorly lubricated stage to do with the knee being too tight and starved of its own juices. These are the knees that click a lot with extremes of movement, such as getting up from your haunches or bending over to pick something up from the floor. They rarely swell and they only feel discomfort when they have stayed too straight or too bunched up for any period of time. In fact, these are the knees of most of us who are over thirty-five, and most of us stay at this stage. They are grumbling knees but nothing disastrous.

More advanced cases are rarer and usually have some previous accident or strain to thank for their downhill slide. In these cases, swelling is an ever-present factor. It is there for two reasons. First, it is the result of irritation of the synovium, the inside lining membrane of the capsule of the knee. The capsule is the sleeve-like soft-tissue wrapping which binds the bones of the joint together.

Within that, the two bone ends float in fluid so the encapsulated knee joint acts like a hydraulic sac, dispersing force in different directions as we stand on the leg. So instead of the bones grinding together as we take weight on them, they are held apart by the pressure of the fluid. We actually float on a cushion of fluid which has oozed out of the synovial membrane. This lubricating membrane pours out fluid when it is irritated, not unlike the mucosal lining of our nose. And because the synovial membrane is in such intimate contact with the capsule of the joint, it will suffer in the same way that the capsule suffers, once it gets too tight. Rather like a knitted woollen sleeve which has shrunk in the wash, the capsule of the knee will lose stretch if the knee suffers a chronic lack of romp and variety of movement. As the knee loses 'play' and closes down, the capsule and its intimate lining of synovium become more and more inelastic and unforgiving. Soon enough, we get adaptive shortening and thickening and it becomes easier and easier to tug and wrench the knee during everyday movement. The damaged membrane pours out fluid into the joint and the knee swells. This is one reason for the swelling.

The second reason occurs during the much more terminal phases of the knee's health. It goes something like this: poor lubrication of the knee results in the hydraulic sac qualities of the knee becoming impaired. Almost as if the bones are wading in a paddling pool, they do not have enough fluid to float in. The bones are more subject to grinding and knocking as the knee works. This is severely testing for the smooth spongy shock-absorbing hyaline cartilage which covers the two opposing bone surfaces for the purpose of facilitating friction-free action. With impaired lubrication, it becomes progressively assaulted chipped and eroded. This lubricating fluid becomes a floating tide of cartilaginous debris within the knee. In order to clean up the joint space and check this self-silting process, the synovial membrane comes to the rescue. It pours into the joint space fluid which contains huge cartilage-eating cells; the more debris to be devoured, the more fluid secreted into the joint. Another reason for the swelling.

— *Irritation of the Kneecap (Chondromalacia patella)* —

This is a specific condition where there is rub between the underneath of the kneecap on the front of the knee. As I said earlier, the kneecap is an anti-friction device which minimises the fraying effect on the tendon as it works like a pulley across the front of the knee joint. In its healthy state, the kneecap floats well forward of the hinge joint which it straddles, only occasionally coming down closer to the moving bones, either when the leg is heavily loaded (for example, when getting up from a chair or walking down a steep slope or downstairs), or when the knee is bunched up into a tight angle. Then the smooth cartilage cover of the underside of the kneecap does its work by lightly glancing off the front of the hinge, thereby deflecting the ominous approach of the angling knee joint.

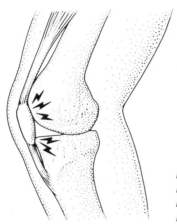

If the knee never fully straightens, there is increased friction of the back of the kneecap against the front of the knee hinge.

Several sets of circumstances can thwart this healthy remoteness with which the kneecap remains at a distance in front of the knee. One has been discussed already; that of creeping angulation of the knee as a fixed contracture or tightness of the knee, so that the front of the knee pokes into the back of the patella. The second is a more widespread general lack of 'looseness' of the knee joint, the result of multiple accessory movement loss. The kneecap rides down too closely on the front of the hinge joint over which it is meant to be the guard. This too means the underside of the kneecap will be scraped; scoured by its drag across the bending knee bones.

There are two further reasons for kneecap scouring: knock-knees and bow-legs. In these cases the angulation between the femur and the tibia thwarts the ability of the kneecap to track true during its excursion around the bend of the knee. The quadriceps tendon will tend to pull the kneecap either diagonally outwards (knock-knees) or diagonally inwards (bow-legs), instead of just upwards. Both conditions set up irritation behind the kneecap.

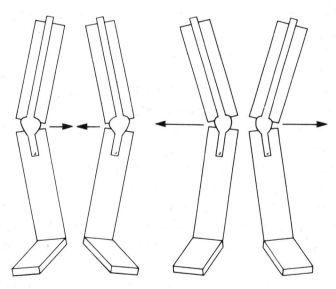

With bow legs (left) the kneecap tends to drag inwards instead of tracking true.

With knock knees (right) it displaces laterally instead of tracking true, as the knee bends and straightens.

Some degree of irritation behind the patella is extremely common. Most of us have a bit of it although usually it takes fairly hefty direct pressure down on the top of the kneecap while the leg is straight, and then attempting to lift the leg, to elicit it. In mild cases, the undersurface of the kneecap will be roughened rather like a splintery board. The knees click a lot, especially as you bend down. Sometimes you can even feel the knee grinding if you feel over the front of the knee while bending and straightening your leg. In severe cases, as observed by arthroscoping inside the knee, the underside of the kneecap can look as if there are trails of seaweed hanging down. These knees are a real problem. The joint can be permanently hot and swollen and there is usually wasting of the quadriceps muscles of the front of the thigh. It is extremely uncomfortable to sit for any length of time with your knee bent. You find it excruciating to have to sit in the cinema or travel in an airline seat and if you have to sit, you try to find a place where you can have your leg outstretched. Probably the worst activity is driving; not only sitting with your knees bunched up under the steering wheel but the vibration of the vehicle, as well as the effort of pressing down the pedals. It is agony to change gear, quite apart from stopping at the lights!

In extreme cases, you will walk with a peculiar gait; with as little knee bend as possible. You need a stick, or maybe two sticks, and you will swing your leg forwards from the hip and then snap it back hard to lock it. You do this to spare yourself the ordeal of using muscle control (of the quadriceps group) to get the leg straight. Characteristically, you would prefer to do anything to avoid walking down slopes and stairs, often going the long way round if a certain set of steps or a ramp is without a handrail. At worst, you may have to go down the steps one at a time, tottering and leading with your bad leg.

Turning or twisting movements, where a sub-clinical irritation of the kneecap has been brewing for a while, may be the catalyst which is your final undoing. Whatever you were doing when you were caught off-guard and swung around, it is entirely possible to end up in a heap on the floor. This is often the beginning of a long history of knee trouble.

WHAT CAN YOU DO ABOUT IT?

Stretch is the answer. With the knee, as with any joint, a certain slackness promotes ongoing health. Looseness keeps it alive; the basic tenet of eternal youth. This means that the knee is less tightly bound, with more room for manoeuvre inside. The increased 'elastic give' of the joint means that the two bones are not so jammed together. The femoral condyles are less constrained into single trammelled tracks across the surface of the tibia, so they do not wear out a pathway as they roll back and forth. Equally important, the knee can get safely back into full lock so there is no wobble.

My advice is to stay the knife. Whatever is wrong, there are subtler, kinder ways of putting them right. If you come to physiotherapists first of all we have to analyse the joint; watch it and feel it for malfunction. This is almost like listening to the joint; gently laying on the hands and sensing the problems through feel. How does the joint respond at the limits of its range – does it bounce or does it thud? Does it have vital accessory freedoms to be got back? But this is not just for the professionals to do: it's much better if you do it yourself.

E X E R C I S E   1

Knee Swings

This is the first and easiest exercise for your knees.

1 Sit yourself up high on a table with an uncluttered space under the table so that your feet can swing freely and like a child perched on a

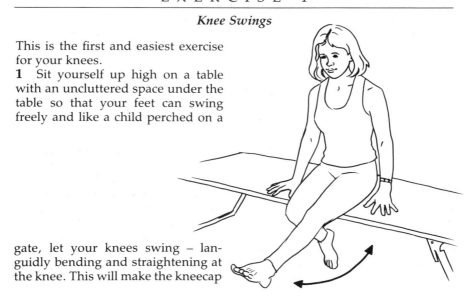

gate, let your knees swing – languidly bending and straightening at the knee. This will make the kneecap glance lightly back and forth over the knee hinge, the gentle friction polishing the roughened under-surface of the kneecap, rather like sandpapering a splintery board.

2 Repeat as often as you like. Even a few minutes a day can make all the difference.

EXERCISE 2

Knee Clenches

1 Sit on the floor with your legs stretched straight out in front of you, hands on the floor behind for support.

2 Clench the thigh muscles of one leg and attempt to raise the back of the heel clear off the floor by pushing the back of the knee hard into the

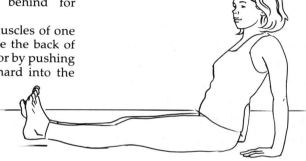

floor. A healthy knee should let the heel lift by about three centimetres (just over an inch).

3 Hold the position for 10 seconds, clenching so hard that your thigh nearly cramps.

4 Repeat four or five times then do the same with the other leg.

EXERCISE 3

The Knee Seesaw

You will need two chairs for this exercise.

1 Kneel on your left knee between the two chairs, resting your right foot flat on the floor in front of you so that the right leg assumes an obtuse angle.

2 With your hands on the chairseats and taking some of your weight through your arms, move for-wards over the left knee so you end up taking most of your weight on your right foot. This will hurt as your full weight passes over your left kneecap. You may need to have some padding like a folded towel under the kneecap if it is too painful.

3 Reverse the movement and then sit back on your left foot with your left knee fully bent.

4 Continue moving back and forth for 2 minutes. As time passes you will notice that the movement becomes less painful.

5 Reverse the position of your legs and repeat the sequence on the other kneecap.

EXERCISE 4

A Child's Squat

You will need a small cushion for this exercise.

1 Kneel on the floor with your knees together and the small cushion between your ankles.

2 Widen the gap between your feet to about thirty centimetres (twelve inches) keeping the upper side of your feet on the floor and your toes pointing straight back.

3 Keeping your knees together lower your bottom down on to the cushion and sit there for 2 minutes. Those of you with loose knees may not need the cushion; others with tighter knees may need more cushions.

4 Ease forwards and take the weight off your feet.

5 Repeat once more.

EXERCISE 5

The Sitting Bowl

This is similar to the previous exercise but you won't need the cushion.

1 Kneel on the floor.

2 Keeping your knees and your big toes pressed together, hook your thumbs around the inner side of each heel and pull them outwards.

3 With the heels as widely separated as possible, lower your bottom down into the bowl-shaped hollow made by your feet.

4 Sit there for 1 minute with your bottom pressing your feet apart.

5 Release and relax and repeat once more.

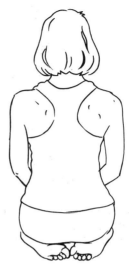

Chapter Thirteen

THE

ANKLES

WHAT IS AN ANKLE?

The ankle complex is an unusual one. It provides lateral stability so that we can balance the foot on the ground. It also
provides a hinge movement so that we can strike the ground
with our heel and proceed through to push-off during the act of
locomotion.

Strictly speaking, the ankle pure is a hinge at the bottom of the
shin which connects the leg to the foot. The two bones of the lower
leg, the tibia (the larger one on the inside) and the fibula (the
narrower one on the outside) make a vice-like mortice which hugs
the uppermost bone of the foot – the talus. Several tarsal bones make
up the middle part of the foot and these stack themselves around in
an arch, at the apex of which sits the talus, ready to be clutched by
the two ankle-bones coming down from above.

Only the tibia makes a weight-bearing contact with the top of the
talus. The fibula sits alongside the outer side of the talus making
glancing contact. Its more important role is making compact the
mortice which houses the talus. The bottom end of the fibula travels
lower down when covering the outside of the ankle joint and if you

look at your own foot you will see that the outer ankle-bone is lower. The tibia on the inside does not extend down so far. Also, the outside ankle-bone sits further back than the inner one; two factors which make it easier for the foot to roll under during injury to the ankle.

The upper weight-bearing surface of the talus is shaped like a dome or hemisphere. As you point your toe, the dome rolls out from under the scooped shelf of the bottom of the tibia. As you bring your foot back towards you, the dome rolls back under the eave of the tibia.

With the talus sitting at the top of the arch of the foot, the rest of the foot spans out below it in a curve. The talus does not sit quite squarely between the two ankle-bones; it has a slight inward attitude as it makes contact with the rest of the foot below. This

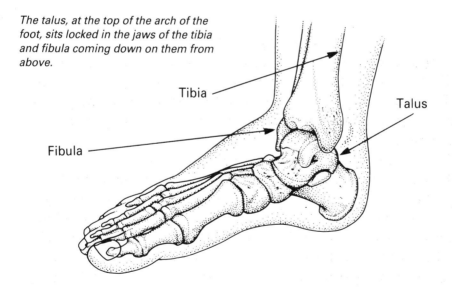

The talus, at the top of the arch of the foot, sits locked in the jaws of the tibia and fibula coming down on them from above.

Tibia

Talus

Fibula

'twisted' orientation of the talus has important ramifications in the malfunction of the sub-talar part of the foot, as we shall see later. The talus bone makes a joint with the heel bone or calcaneum which sits below it and further back; and with the navicular, in front of it and below. From the navicular, the foot distributes stress downwards into the calcaneum of the heel and forwards and downwards through the arch and to the metatarsal bones. The metatarsal bones fan out across the front of the foot from the block of tarsal bones. They are five fine long bones which, in their relatively loose parallel union to one another, give the forefoot fantastic lateral pliability. The toes attach to the front of the foot at their junction with the metatarsals, and continue on beyond to give extra stability and propulsion. The ideal forefoot bears most of its weight on the head of the first metatarsal where it joins with the big toe, and at the head of the fifth metatarsal where it joins with the little toe. The heel at the back bears over half our weight and the forefoot shares the rest. Poorly functioning feet bear weight on all the metatarsal heads instead of just the outer two (see the next chapter for more information).

How Does the Ankle Work?

The only movement between the bottom of the leg and the talus is the simple nodding up and down movement; a rolling action of the talus between the two ankle-bones. The inwards and outwards movements of the foot take place where the bony arch slides around under the talus. And it is the amalgam of movements which provides the sensationally effective balance as the foot joins the semi-rigid leg to the ground.

The squashing forces transmitted through the top of the bony arch are phenomenal and at all points in the arch, muscles and ligaments have to work in harmony to keep the vault of the foot held high. As you will see in the next chapter, the muscles that work the toes play a major role in keeping the bottom of the arch pinched together, like the catgut across a bow. However, because of the mechanical disadvantage involved, it is not so easy to dissipate the squashing pressure, the nearer one gets to the crest of the arch. This is where the dynamics of the talus, the keystone of the arch, come in.

Two muscles help dramatically in keeping the top of the arch up. They have a curious action because neither directly targets the talus, the brick at the very top of the stack; they target the next ones down

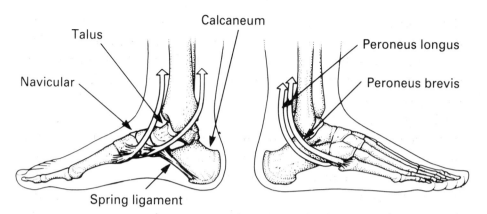

Talus

Navicular

Calcaneum

Peroneus longus

Peroneus brevis

Spring ligament

The spring ligament passes from the calcaneum to the navicular and keeps the talus pinched high.

Peroneus longus and peroneus brevis stabilise the outside of the ankle and help suspend the arch.

and forward in the arch, particularly the navicular. The first muscle is tibialis anterior which is that long fleshy muscle just to the outside of the shinbone in our lower leg. It runs down and crosses the front of the ankle on the inner side. If you bring the inside undersole of your foot up and at the same time bring your toes back towards you, you will see the strong cable of the tibialis anterior tendon webbing the skin up at the inner side of the front of the ankle. The tendon then

The cross-over of tibialis posterior and peroneus longus acts like an elastic stirrup suspending the arch of the foot and keeping the foot flat on the floor.

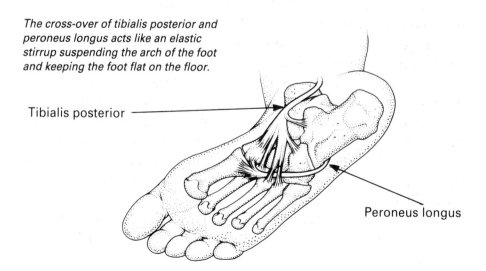

Tibialis posterior

Peroneus longus

continues across the top of the foot and attaches into the top of the arch of the forefoot – into the first cuneiform, in front of the navicular, and then the first metatarsal. By attaching here it tugs upwards at the top of the crescent and keeps the inner arch of the foot held high.

The second muscle is its sister muscle, the tibialis posterior, which is also discussed in the next chapter on feet. This comes down from the back of the thigh, hooks around the inside ankle-bone and approaches the navicular bone from the underside of the foot. Although it approaches the same bone (the navicular) from the opposite direction from the tibialis anterior, it also succeeds in pinching the sides of the arch together and keeping the vault of the foot high. You can identify this muscle by pointing the toes downwards while at the same time turning the foot in and lifting the inside border of it up towards you. So to summarise, the difference in their actions is as follows: tibialis anterior hauls the top of the arch up from above, while tibialis posterior, by pulling the navicular bone down and back towards the heel, pinches the sides of the arch into a more acute peak. Sensational! Two strong and dominant muscles, competently sharing the role of keeping the body weight from flattening the top of the inner arch of the foot; one muscle which works when the toe is pointed and the other which works when the toes and foot are cocked back towards you – each when the foot is turned in.

There is one final thing to say about the maintenance of the top of the arch of the mid-foot and that is the role of the spring ligament. This is a small, relatively insignificant but fantastically strong ligament at the top of the bony arch of the foot. It spans the gulf between the calcaneum and the navicular, running underneath the talus. It has a similar function to that of the tibialis posterior mentioned above, but it works under different conditions. The spring ligament comes into its own when we land heavily on the foot, like we do when jumping, running, hopping or skipping, when the muscles alone could not cope. By its tugging resilience it prevents the two bones which flank the talus below from separating when the foot has to tolerate sudden and excessive downwards force. The muscles operate more continuously, exerting a low-grade tension to keep the arch high, relying on the spring ligament in moments of stress to prevent the arch smashing apart and the talus imploding through to the floor. Its strength keeps the apex of the arch pinched into an acute peak, the talus staying propped atop at the pinnacle.

WHAT ARE THE ACCESSORY MOVEMENTS OF THE ANKLE?

You might wonder why I am making all this fuss about the maintenance of the upper echelons of the bony arch of the foot. It is all to do with the incremental hidden movements made by the talus during the act of weight-bearing – since the talus is the keystone of the arch. I said at the outset that the talus does not move except in an up-and-down hinging movement, but that is not strictly so. It has a small but vital component of accessory movement which makes all the difference to the ability of the arch to absorb shock. As weight comes over the foot there is a slight nodding twisting movement of the talus as it moves inwards and downwards; a sort of a screwing action. This screw action is an ingenious way of dissipating force. It is the initial move from the top of the arch down in the dispersing of weight through the foot. It causes a slight rolling-in action over the inner border of the foot as the arch flattens out with pressure. At the same time, because the forefoot is flat along the floor, there is a relative twisting action between the mid-foot and the forefoot; only slight but there. As soon as the weight comes off, the arch comes up and the foot de-rotates and becomes straight again. Look down at your own bare foot as you walk and you will see this happening. As your weight comes over, there is a momentary bulge of your mid-foot along the inner border of your foot, quite high up near the inner ankle-bone. At the same time, the calcaneum tilts slightly inwards as the weight comes over the foot. These small movements of the talus and the calcaneum are but two of the accessory movements which help the foot absorb shock but they can also get out of control, go too far and can't get back, and we will look at this later.

The other accessory movements of the ankle which are important are those that take place under the talus; between the talus and the rest of the foot. Sub-talar movement allows the greater part of the inwards and outwards swivel action of the foot. Without it, we would have very little lateral tolerance of the foot on the ground with the risk of injury when walking on uneven surfaces. You can demonstrate this movement for yourself. Sit with your right lower leg on top of your left knee and hold the front of the right lower leg/ankle with your right hand; index and middle fingers spreading down over the front of the ankle crease to stabilise the talus. Now, with your left hand cupped around your right heel, waggle the heel inwards and outwards on the leg. (You will feel the dome of the talus wobbling under the fingers of your right hand as you do it.) This lateral movement of the foot is the sub-talar movement and you will notice that there is more inwards movement than there is outwards. This can lead to trouble. For the foot to be able to balance the skeleton, it is vital that it retains the full complement of sub-talar freedom.

You can also see that a deficiency of talar freedom, the first accessory movement discussed, will have some effect on the freedom of these sub-talar movements. Indeed one group of accessory movements directly influences the other.

How Does the Ankle Go Wrong?

Both the congenital configurations of the bones of the feet, as well as acquired weakness of the supporting musculature of the feet can lead to trouble with the ankles.

If you are born with an unusually short first metatarsal, this can set off the downwards slide in the function of the ankles. It means that too much weight is borne by the head of the second metatarsal as the weight rolls over the forefoot and on to push-off when walking. As a result, the muscles which work the big toe will become weaker. Since these same muscles also help in suspending the long inner arch of the foot, the arch also becomes weak and starts to drop. The critical point here is that as the arch drops it drags in with it the front of the talus. This is just like the transient action of the talus during the weight-bearing phase of walking, when the arch temporarily flattens, except that this time it is for keeps; as weight leaves the foot, the talus does not spring back. Over time, the front of the talus turns further and further in and down and the arch insidiously drops. Neither the two prime movers, tibialis anterior and posterior, nor the spring ligament, can stop the mid-foot from rolling down and inwards. The mechanical strain on the muscles and ligaments is too great. Over time they all become attenuated and weak and the foot flattens. At the same time, the foot twists between the mid-foot and the forefoot, as discussed earlier as a temporary phenomenon.

The progressive deforming of the foot is further hastened by the action of another muscle, the peroneus brevis. This muscle passes down around the outside ankle-bone and along the outside of the foot to the base of the fifth metatarsal, about half-way along the outside of the foot. By its tension, it suspends the lower and less important lateral arch of the foot but as the weak instep progressively falls inwards, the action of the peroneus brevis deforms the foot even more. It twists the foot by pulling outwards on the outside of the forefoot, as the mid-foot rolls in the other way. Its continued tension in the face of such feeble reciprocal control by the two tibialis muscles on the inside of the ankle makes a harmless normal muscle become an added persecutor. You will see at the end of this chapter that Exercise 4 (The Foot Twist) reverses this condition by stretching the tight outer border of the foot while at the same time re-establishing the inner arch.

The next set of factors which can affect the ankle working properly all lie in the anatomical design of the foot. They seem to predispose the ankle to harm by turning itself under in the classical twisting-under strain of the ankle. This is perhaps the commonest ankle injury.

First, when your foot is at rest – off the ground and not bearing weight – it assumes a languid in-looking attitude with the soles of the feet seeming to face one another. Have a look at this with your own. Secondly, its natural range of movement is more in the inward

155

direction than outward (as we saw above when waggling our own ankle to demonstrate sub-talar movement). Thirdly, from the point of view of the bones there seems to be a bias towards the foot rolling inwards. For a start, the length of the metatarsals and toes tapers back from the front of the foot to the outer side, making it easier for the foot to roll over on its outer edge. And the length of the 'cover' of the two ankle-bones as they extend down either side of the talus also has its contribution to make. The fact that the outer one, the fibula, is not only longer but also situated further back than the inner one, also makes it harder for the foot to twist outwards than inwards.

All these factors lumped together do have a purpose. They help give the inside arch of the foot more gumption than the outer one, something that is vital to the properties of stress distribution and the action of push-off in the foot. In its natural state, the foot is almost pulled around into an inwards concavity or crescent which increases the power of the inner arch to resist flattening and also helps to make the big toe and, to a lesser degree, the second toe the chief orchestrators of push-off. It can, however, lead to trouble as far as accidental injury is concerned.

THE COMMON DISORDERS OF THE ANKLES

Simply speaking, there are two sets of circumstances which commonly afflict the ankle, both related to the anomalies of accessory movement described above: first, the developmental falling inwards of the mid-foot in the manner described above; and secondly, the propensity of the outer side of the foot to suffer injury in the traumatic twisting under of the ankle. Both sets of circumstances are directly related to poor muscle control, although it is true that the bony configuration of the foot may be the catalyst in the works.

——— *Sagging Inner Arches of the Mid-foot* ———

This is a common enough problem and although it looks unsightly it need not be responsible for a great deal of pain. It is its effects on the arches, especially at the front of the foot, which cause all the pain.

People who have this problem will roll in on their shoes so that the inner side, especially at the back of the shoe, becomes stretched and distorted and the inside heel will be worn down. If you look at the unshod feet from behind, you will see the heels splaying out under the ankles, with the inner ankle-bones so close they almost touch while the heels remain widely separated. The condition becomes painful if it is associated with marked flattening of the long medial arch of the foot and more particularly of the transverse arch at the front of the foot (see the following chapter on feet).

As a rule, one tends to go with the other – the ankle and the arch distortion – but the ankle in-rolling alone has wider ramifications throughout the skeleton as a whole. Most particularly, it affects the low back. This is for several reasons, not least the impaired ability of the feet to absorb shock which immediately transmits to the lumbar area. But more subtly, it affects the attitude or 'sit' of the pelvis which in turn discommodes the working spine. The in-rolling of the arch tends to swivel the leg inwards and at the same time causes the front of the hips to kink slightly. This then causes the pelvis to tip forwards and a scooped hollow to develop in the low back. Some back disorders can be directly related to this ankle problem, particularly those which are resistant to therapeutic efforts. If the arch in-rolling is particularly advanced we use orthotics (custom-designed insoles) in the shoes to correct the flattening. These are made by podiatrists or physiotherapists and, by wedging up the inner border of the foot, they help to unravel the back problem from the feet upwards. (You will see in the next chapter on feet that this disorder can be fed from either end – either the hips not having enough 'turn out' which leads to the arches dropping or the arches dropping as the primary flaw which leads to the hips turning in, as in the manner described above.)

157

The Chronically Twisting Ankle

Although this is not a degenerative condition *per se* – it starts off with a twisting injury to the ankle – it tends to become a chronic disorder because of the gradual deterioration of the ankle's function. It always begins with an accidental wrenching of the ankle when the weight comes down on the outside border of the foot and the foot buckles under at the sub-talar joint. If the first injury is very severe it rarely heals properly. And it is possibly this injury, especially in its chronic or long-term form, that best illustrates the way hidden malfunction at one of the composite joints of a system can lead first to recurrent injury and then to worsening of the original condition, and eventually to incorporating all the joints in the system.

Take the first injury. The mechanics of this strain are this: the subtle inwards movement of the foot under the talus is forced to extremes by the body weight coming down hard on the foot in its twisted-under position. The immediate joint strain induced, with its stretching of fibres and local painful swelling, sets up a reaction where the surrounding muscles temporarily 'lock down' the injured joint to take it out of action.

The only trouble with this automatic joint-locking facility (known as protective muscle spasm) is that, in terms of a quick resolution of the problems, this is really the last thing that the joint needs. Ideally, for the sake of the future health of the joint, it is better that this swelling is pumped away by the body as soon as possible, since if it lies around in the tissues it will stagnate and form scar tissue. Sadly, when caught in the hold of over-zealous muscle protection (often added to by anxiety and apprehension of the sufferer), the ankle finds itself caught in exactly such scar tissue; a web of its own making. After the pain has gone and even though it might want to move normally, it finds it cannot because it is tethered by its own tight structures. And this is how the plot thickens. The ankle cannot move freely during everyday movement and when it comes to the inwards movement, the one which first suffered the strain, it finds it painful and restricted. Eventually, this inwards movement is completely lost. There is no inwards glide of the foot underneath the talus, and even the slightest hint of your ankle wanting to turn under will make you collapse with the pain. Even getting your foot sideways, half off an uneven paving stone, can be enough to make you go down. You go through the whole catastrophe again: marked puffy swelling, acute tenderness over the outside of the ankle, wincing pain even as you go to lift the foot off the floor and, of course, an impossible limp – crutches with the foot hanging down limply with the knee bent and the toes puffy, even blue. When you rest the sore foot you will lay it out on the floor in front of you. It will have passively assumed a pointed-toe attitude and, as you lift it off the ground, you cannot bear to lift the toes of the foot back first. Small as this movement is, it tends to stress the outside of the foot which causes pain.

From here on it is a slow road to get the ankle working properly again. If not treated adequately in the first instance, one episode inevitably leads to the next. Sooner or later the ankle is so handicapped by the snowballing problem that other movements start to wane. Again, the domino effect.

The most striking feature of this type of ankle is its chronic state of thickness. Unlike the other ankle which looks fine and delicately turned in comparison, this one is leathery and solid and lacking in its multiple curves and contours. If you test it, you find that most of its movements are difficult. It lacks range in the action of pointing the toe, just as much as the opposite movement; bringing the toes back towards you. Most particularly, it finds it cannot glide inwards, the heel under the rest of the foot. However, it is the sub-talar movement in combination with all the other tarsal and metatarsal movements which really demonstrate the loss. This is done by twisting the whole foot under and you can do this yourself on a normal foot. Sit as you did before with your right foot up on your left knee. Grab the front of your forefoot up near the toes with both hands and twist the forefoot around so that you can see most of the sole of your foot. Apply quite a lot of pressure and take it around until you feel the pain start to bite. On a normal foot this will be quite a long way, but if you have problems with sub-talar freedom there will be hardly any inwards movement before you are stopped by pain.

But it is the pattern of repeated twisting episodes that sets this problem apart from others. It seems that once you have the problem you keep on redoing it; the good ankle never seems to come in for the same sort of trauma as the bad. As you know, it is the clenching-out of accessory movement and the resulting lack of passive acceptance of the jolts and bangs of everyday life which sets this joint up and makes it vulnerable to injury: a walking accident waiting to happen. And it is only by restoring full accessory freedom that this joint can return to the fold of normality.

WHAT CAN YOU DO ABOUT IT?

Again, like all joints the path to restoration follows the same sign-posts: restore universal joint freedom to the ankle complex and strengthen the muscle weakness, if there is any. Broadly speaking lack of up and down freedom of the foot at the ankle influences our walking; it limits our length of stride and the efficiency of push off. On the other hand, paucity of lateral freedom at the ankle undermines our ability to balance and the ability of our foot to maintain its arches.

EXERCISE 1

The Foot Squash

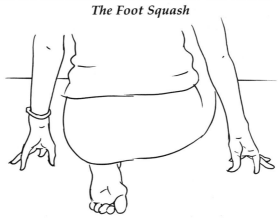

1 Kneel on your left knee with your right leg out in front of you, its foot flat on the floor.
2 Balancing with your fingertips on the floor, lower your weight down on to the point of your heel and sit on it. Make sure your foot does not roll inwards or outwards and keep your toes pointing straight back.
3 Sit like that for 2 minutes then release.
4 Reverse your position and repeat with the other foot.

EXERCISE 2

The Achilles Stretch

1 Stand on a stair facing up the staircase. Hold on to a banister if possible. If you don't have stairs find a step of at least ten centimetres drop (four inches).

2 Stand right at the front edge of the stair, literally hanging on with your toes, and let your heels sink down to the next level. In your efforts to bring your heels down, don't let your bottom poke out. You will feel a pulling sensation at the back of your calves as you hang there.

3 Hold the position for 30 seconds and then rise up again.

4 Repeat four times.

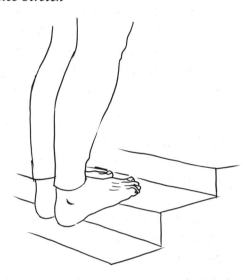

EXERCISE 3

The Crossed-Sole Stretch

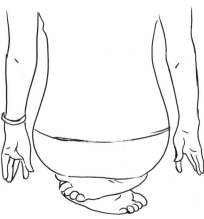

1 Kneel on the floor.

2 Turn the left foot inwards and lay the outside border of the foot along the ground.

3 Place the top of the right forefoot into the saddle of the undersole of the left foot, so that the feet are crossed.

4 Sit back on your feet so that the weight of your bottom pushes your heels, particularly your right heel, outwards.

5 Hold this position for 1 minute then release by easing forwards and taking weight off your feet.

6 Reverse the position of the feet and repeat the sequence.

EXERCISE 4

The Foot Twist

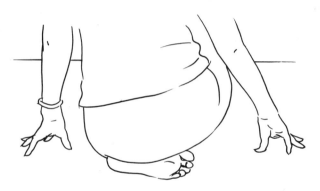

1 Kneel on your left knee with your right leg out in front of you, its foot flat on the floor.

2 Turn the toes of your left foot inwards and lay the outside border of this foot along the floor behind you, that ankle at a right angle.

3 Lower your bottom down on to the inside border of your left foot, especially the inner heel. Take some of your body weight through your arms. Depending on how much weight you let down, the ankle will be pushed to a greater or lesser degree into an inwards position.

4 Hold this position for 1 minute and then release by leaning forwards and easing off the foot.

5 Repeat once then change sides and repeat the sequence with the other foot.

EXERCISE 5

Ankles-Touching Tiptoes

This is harder than it looks.

1 Stand in front of a mantelpiece or hand-basin and hold on with your index finger – more to steady yourself than to take weight.

2 Keep your feet close together and your ankle-bones touching and raise yourself high on to your toes.

3 Hold that position for 1 minute without letting your heels fall apart then lower yourself back down again.

4 Repeat once. Hard isn't it?

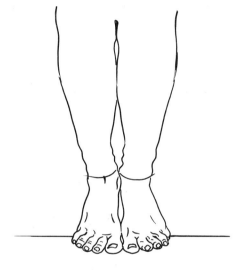

163

Chapter Fourteen

THE FEET

WHAT IS A FOOT?

The foot is a sensationally structured mobile arch which connects the bottom of the semi-rigid leg to the earth. In many ways the arch resembles the sweeping curves of an old Roman bridge; the sandstone blocks of the bridge stacking around the arch, their sheer weight and falling-together pressure providing the stability of the curve. The shape of the bones of the foot fit together to make a natural arch. In fact, there is not just one arch but three. There is the obvious one, the one down the inside border of the foot, a lesser one down the outer side of the foot from the front of the heel to the base of the little toe. And there is also a transverse arch, across the front of the foot between the base of the big toe and the little toe.

The foot has five metatarsal bones which fan out across the front of the foot in front of the tarsals, the collection of bones of the mid-foot. They spread forwards like a chicken's claw on the ground and connect up with the toes which in turn continue on beyond the sole of the foot. The calcaneum or heel-bone sits behind the arch and during normal standing takes a little over half the weight of the

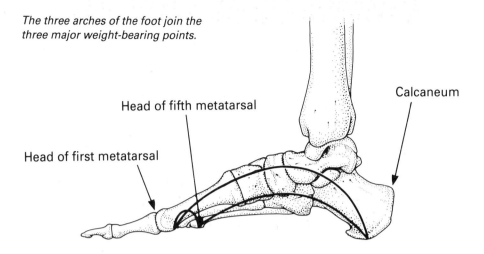

The three arches of the foot join the three major weight-bearing points.

Head of fifth metatarsal

Calcaneum

Head of first metatarsal

body. The rest of the body weight is then shared between the front end of the first metatarsal (which connects to the big toe) and the front end of the fifth metatarsal (which connects to the little toe). Ideally, there will be minimal weight borne by the area between, especially under the base of the second toe which, being at the peak of the transverse arch, sits the highest off the floor. The three arches of the foot connect the three points of weight bearing.

The arches are everything to a foot; without them a foot would not be a foot. Not only would we find it impossible to stand there dispersing the body's weight but we would find we had no shock absorption when we walk and no spring in our step during the push-off phase of walking.

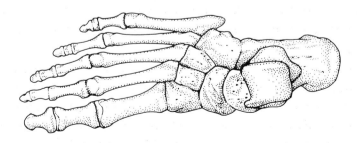

The foot spreads over the floor like a claw.

How Does a Foot Work?

The foot largely works because of the toes, those funny little projections off the front of the feet. We don't use them much these days, wrapping them up and pushing them into shoes all the time. But if our toes work well, so do our feet.

The most obvious job of the toes is to grab the ground and push us forwards and let loose they will do that very well. But they can do more. You only have to see thalidomide children manipulating objects with their feet to see that toes are blessed with far greater reserves of function than we ever call upon them to use. Indeed, they have exactly the same musculature as the hands. There may be no opposing thumb but even so, feet are nearly as useful as hands when they have to be.

However potentially useful the feet might be, we usually only demand two jobs of them: weight distribution and locomotive push-off. The toes contribute substantially to both functions because the toes and the arches are intimately related. The muscles which work the toes, making them claw the floor to push us forwards also help bow the arch upwards and stop it flattening down when bearing weight.

Having said that, it is not *just* the muscles of the toes which keep the arches up. Muscles of the calf also have their contribution to make. In particular, the tibialis posterior and the peroneus longus make an input which is less vulnerable to the whimsy of the way we use our toes. Both these muscles originate high in the back of the calf. One passes down on the inside of the ankle and the other on the outside but their important contribution to arch maintenance comes when they both cross under the sole of the foot like a stirrup.

Tibialis posterior turns the foot in. It hooks around behind the inside ankle-bone and enters the underside of the foot at the top of the medial arch. It runs forwards in a diagonal direction towards the little toe, sending out multiple strands of attachment to the bones in the area as it goes (see the illustration on page 151 in the previous chapter on ankles). The other muscle, peroneus longus, turns the foot out. It approaches from the other direction; swinging around under the outside ankle-bone and also sending out multiple strands of attachment, it runs diagonally forwards across the underneath of the foot towards the big toe. As one set of fibres passes over the top of the other, they form a cross-hatching of muscle fibres. As they contract and tighten, the muscular lattice slings both the inner and the transverse arch of the foot upwards.

In short, the cross-over effect of this muscular duo performs several functions. It keeps the ankle steady on the floor so that it doesn't develop a lateral wobble. It suspends both arches of the foot – tibialis posterior the inner arch, and peroneus longus the transverse arch – and it also aligns the foot so that the big toe and the second toe do most of the push-off during walking. A marvellous co-operative effort, don't you think?

Broadly speaking, there are two sets of muscles which work the toes in grabbing the earth. First, there are the long flexors which come down from the back of the calf and span the underside of the foot to the toes. They curl the toes under, particularly the big toe, in a scrunching action. Secondly, there are the smaller, shorter toe flexors called the intrinsics. These originate under the foot and go through to the toes. They have a different action. They pull the toes to the floor and at the same time keep them straight; only bending the joint where the toe joins the foot, rather like the action of the fingers when playing the piano.

As we walk, we swing the non-weight-bearing leg through and strike the ground with the heel. Ideally, after heel-strike, our weight rolls straight forwards along the foot, over the mid-foot and on to the ball of the foot to the toes. At push-off, we claw the ground in a straight-toed action, mainly with the great toe and the second toe – correct ankle stabilisation having aligned the foot so that it is able to do this.

A footprint in the sand reveals all there is to know about a foot. A perfectly balanced and dynamic foot leaves a finely-etched scooped-out print but a severely dysfunctional foot will leave a great pad of a print, just like Yeti, the abominable snowman. The perfect foot leaves a delicately sculptured print, easily reflecting the three heaviest points of contact on the ground: a deeper impression under the heel; a less deep one under the base of the great toe, and a shallower one at the base of the little toe. Incidentally, you can always tell if the prints in the sand are from someone who has been running because the indentations at the toes will be deeper from the increased power of push-off.

What are the Accessory Movements of the Feet?

The important accessory freedom of the feet is the fine interplay between the several small composite bones which make up the arch of the foot. The tension of the ligaments across the sole of the foot as well as the power of the muscles acting across the breach, offset the flattening effect of the body weight bearing down on the top of the arch. With each step we take, the arch flattens slightly to absorb the shock of the load. But as we start to push off, the arches are pinched together again by the muscles of the toes clawing the ground and by the elastic-stirrup effect of the calf muscles working around the ankle.

This means that during normal walking (taking weight alternately from foot to foot and then pushing off into the swing phase as the non-weight-bearing leg is carried through), the arch of the foot raises and lowers like the Sydney Harbour bridge bowing up and flattening its famous arch. For this to happen there must be good mobility between all the bones of the foot, particularly the middle foot. The bones must all be free to ride up and down independently of one another, rather like linked pontoons floating on a swell. The bones must be free to open away from one another along the underside of the arch, forming V-shaped divots as the foot flattens. Internal mobility is also needed in a lateral spread across the foot so that the sole of the foot can mould itself to uneven surfaces on the ground in the same way that the palm of the hand can mould Plasticine.

The more mobile the foot the better. The more the individual bones can jostle and glide in relation to one another the more adaptable the foot will be. If accessory movement tightens up and the foot becomes semi-rigid, then the dynamic arch qualities of the foot will suffer. As the arches collapse, a terrible saga can set in. The pain on walking, even standing, is an eternal lament.

Just as important is the effect on the rest of the body. If the arch is rigid, the shock-absorption qualities of the foot will be impaired. The ramifications from this travel far afield from the feet. If the feet slap the ground and there is no gentle letting down of the body weight, the entire skeletal frame will be shocked. The juddering can be felt right throughout the body; every joint will jump. The skeleton and its joints are prematurely aged.

How Does a Foot Go Wrong?

Binding the feet in socks and cramming them into shoes is one of the worst things you can do. This locks the toes away from usefulness and starts the steady decline. We should spend as much time as possible without shoes and socks on, just so that the toes can be free to participate and our arches can have a better chance of staying up. Imagine how useless our hands would be if they were encased in mittens all day.

But the toes! Entombed under all that leather, they are kept away from the warm earth. They never reach the ground. They cannot hook their farthest toe-pads around humps in the ground and they are not allowed to participate in getting us about. In truth, we hardly notice the deficit when wearing shoes. In fact, we quite like it. Life is made so easy for us with most of our walking surfaces dead-flat and steps provided wherever there is a slope; we hardly notice the lack of grip our toes might give.

But the foot suffers. Weakness of the intrinsic muscles of the feet immediately affects the toes and the arches. With the straightening action of the intrinsics removed the toes start to claw. Unrestrained, the muscles which curl the toes under and the ones which lift the toes back make it impossible for the toes to remain straight. Instead of lying flat along the floor they scrunch up above the level of the rest of the foot in a hooked fashion and, even when walking bare-footed, they barely reach down to the ground. The toes have completely lost

169

their function of gripping the ground. Often there are calluses on the top of the toes where the angled joint of the toe rubs against the inner surface of the shoes. When the shoe pushes the toes down, they are forced to bear weight on the tip of the toe, even the nail, instead of the proper toe-pad on the undersurface. More importantly, the arches drop. This has all sorts of far-reaching side effects, not least unsightly feet and at worst, crippling pain.

THE COMMON DISORDERS OF THE FEET
Flat Feet

When the long arch on the inside of the foot falls, it is usually associated with a defect of ankle control with the result that there is an in-rolling of the mid-foot. This was discussed in detail in the chapter on ankles. Here I will concentrate on the simplest manifestation of dysfunctional feet – flattening of the arches.

Fallen arches are the scourge of the feet. Apart from looking bad, they can be almost unbearably painful. Every step can be agony. As the arch presses down it causes a tired drawing and stinging pain along the inner side of the feet as more weight is borne along the inside border. It is painful to be on your feet for long, especially for periods of standing around without much sprightly walking about.

The flattening of the transverse arch of the foot can be more painful. It is a different sort of pain and feels almost as if you are standing on a stone, right under the middle of the ball of your foot. The whole forefoot is in direct contact with the floor, in particular the front end of the second metatarsal. Unlike the metatarsals for the big toe and the little toe, the head of this metatarsal is not designed to bear weight. It is completely ill-equipped. Most particularly, it doesn't have a fat pad underneath to cushion the contact of the bone with the ground and as a consequence it feels exactly as if you are walking on the bone itself. Over time, thick calluses of skin build up where the second metatarsal head hits the ground, and this makes it even harder for this toe to reach the ground during walking. In extreme cases, the second toe lifts right off the floor, often resting cocked up on the others while the great toe deviates across and rests on the floor beneath it.

Problems of both the medial and the transverse arches can be much exacerbated by women wearing high heels, especially if the shoe also has a very narrow toe. Even if the foot works well enough unshod, it will be completely disabled by the architecture of a shoe of this kind. A couple of factors go towards making the shoe the disaster that it is: the height of the heel and the business of pushing the great toe in and over towards the others. The height of the heel tips the body forwards and puts more weight on the front of the foot. As well as this, the bunching together of the toes in the cramped front of the shoe completely disables the toes from participating in push-off. As a result there is an enforced lapse in the muscle control which suspends the transverse arch, just at the time it is needed more than ever – when more weight than usual is coming down on to the ball of the foot. The transverse arch is flattened and a good proportion of body weight is taken on the head of the second metatarsal. Even in the course of one shopping expedition or one cocktail party, it quickly registers pain; typically as if you are walking on a stone.

Another factor contributes to the flattening of the arches of the feet; that of the hips not having enough 'turn out'. This is a ballet expression which describes the lack of ability of the legs to swivel out at the hips so that, when standing, the feet splay outwards. If the hips have restricted turn out, it is indeed likely that their resting attitude is one of slight 'turn in', with the feet pigeon-toed. The hips also bend slightly and the stance is knock-kneed with a flattening of the long inner arch of the foot.

The in-toeing that occurs with a pigeon-toed gait specifically handicaps the action of the important peroneus longus muscle. You will remember that this muscle not only turns the foot out but also keeps the transverse arch up. Equally so, it keeps the foot straight along the ground during walking so that most of the push-off is done by the great toe and the second toe. Failure of the peroneus longus muscle to work properly during walking lets the foot down in every respect. In summary, a pigeon-toed gait lets both the

171

medial and the transverse arch drop. The specific purpose of Exercise 5 (Ankles-Touching Tiptoes) at the end of the previous chapter is to re-establish power of the peroneus longus muscle. It is as well, when doing all the exercises for the feet, to combine them with all the exercises for the ankles.

Bunions

These are knob-like thickenings at the base of the great toe. One can inherit the propensity to form bunions or they can be the result of wearing bad shoes with a tight or pointed toe, or a very high heel. If you inherit the condition you will be born with an unusually short first metatarsal, the one which connects with the big toe. The second metatarsal is normally only slightly longer than the first but in this case it is much longer – and this brings about bunions.

Several things happen: first, the second metatarsal head, by being too long, collects too much of the brunt of weight-bearing during push-off. This hurts the bone and in time leads to progressive dysfunction of the foot. The big toe gets weaker and this immediately invites further trouble: the atrophy of the small muscles controlling the great toe results in the medial arch and transverse arches dropping even faster. Eventually you have a very unhappy foot, doing most of its weight-bearing and push-off from the middle part of the foot under the second metatarsal head. Painful calluses develop but more worrying is what happens to the big toe. It bends further and further in towards the other toes, at the same time making an unsightly bump along the inside border of the foot where the toe makes an angle with the first metatarsal. The big toe can even ride up over or go under the second toe, by which stage you have a severely dysfunctional foot. There is pain from the bunion itself but there is also pain from the progressive collapsing of the arches.

The cycle fuels itself some more: as the big toe gets more helpless, the muscles controlling it get weaker and weaker. Like perishing catgut across the bow, the weak intrinsic muscles of the transverse arch allow it to drop and as a result the forefoot splays out across the floor. Tight-fitting shoes then play their role; over-correcting the splay of the forefoot by pressing the front of the great toe across into the others. So you can see that bunions can be initiated by the congenital shortness of the first metatarsal but can also develop as the final outcome when the transverse arch of the foot collapses.

In extreme cases, getting shoes to fit is a major problem. The large bump at the base of the great toe is almost impossible to accommodate. Flat sandal-like affairs with an open-laced upper are the most comfortable but you may be able to make do with a normal shoe with bits of leather cut out.

And then there are calluses. These are hard and leathery layers of skin which build up in response to pressure or friction. Calluses under the second metatarsal head are usually the most worrying. The thicker the skin gets, the more they hurt and often relief can only be gained by having them pared down by a chiropodist. Without an understanding of foot mechanics, you may assume that the calluses are the primary problem, and of course this is not so. They will never go away until the function of the foot has been improved.

173

It is awful to see someone with severe bunions trying to walk. They have a painful, hesitating totter. They try to stay back on their heels and take very small steps in a high-stepping action to obviate the need for push-off. They need reams of cotton-wool wadding and corn pads to alleviate pressure areas inside their shoes. But really, the padding is a feeble solution to a sometimes desperate problem. Neither shoes, chiropodists nor padding is the answer. The trick is, remote as the hope might be, to get the toes and the feet working again.

Of course, one hopes that nobody's feet ever deteriorate to this degree. With better understanding and better footwear, it is uncommon these days to see feet this bad. But at the other end of the spectrum – for any normal mortal – better well-being can be had by simply having better feet. Reflexologists even claim that all the body organs have representations over different parts of the soles of the feet. They say that the workings of all our internal organs can be optimised by attention to the feet; that well-working feet make for a well-working system. It is certainly true that high-performance feet make an enormous difference so, whatever the current state of your feet, why not have them better?

WHAT CAN YOU DO ABOUT IT?

One of the first things you can do is take your shoes off more often. The toes rejoice at having all this freedom, and while initially they remain scrunched up in the air, hardly getting any purchase on the ground with each step, sooner than you would think they will try to incorporate into a normal walking pattern. Uneven surfaces help; like soft squashy grass. And while you are walking make a deliberate effort to get the toes down, even to grab the floor, and MAKE them propel you along.

Now for the specific yoga procedures you can do.

E X E R C I S E 1

Arching The Foot

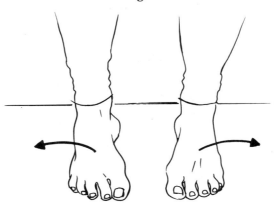

1 Stand upright with your feet parallel and about ten centimetres (four inches) apart.
2 Lift all your toes off the floor and try to separate them.
3 Place them back on the floor keeping them as widely spaced as possible.

4 Grasp the floor with your toes, keeping them straight and not letting them scrunch up, and lift the inside borders of your feet to raise the inner arches.
5 Hold this position for 15 seconds and release.
6 Repeat six times.

EXERCISE 2

The Toes Push-Back

1 Kneel on the floor on your hands and knees.
2 Lean forwards on your hands and turn the tops of your toes under so that the toe-pads are on the floor.
3 Sit back on the turned-under toes for 30 seconds.
4 Release and repeat the sequence three times.

EXERCISE 3

The Toes Push-Under

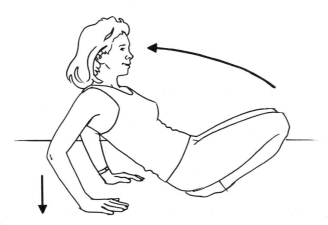

1 Kneel on the floor and sit back on your feet, this time with the top surface of the feet under you on the floor.
2 Place the hands on the floor beside you and, using them to push off, lift your knees as high as possible off the floor, pivoting on the front of your feet and the toes.
3 Rock back as far as you can go, and release.
4 Repeat four times.

EXERCISE 4

The Dowling Torture

You will need a long stick such as a broomstick, a walking stick or a piece of dowling 1.5 centimetre (half an inch) in thickness. It's worth buying dowling especially for this exercise.

1 Stand in front of a mantelpiece or a table or any surface that you can lean on to take weight. Have the stick on the floor in front of you.

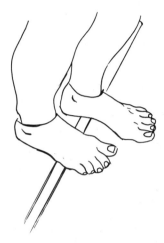

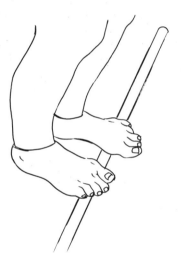

2 Taking some of your weight through your arms, hook your toes over the stick and then incrementally creep forwards, walking over the dowling. Take the smallest possible steps until you have passed right on over the dowling and stepped off the other side. Don't speed up when the dowling is under the painful parts of the foot.

Before beginning this regime please read pages 19 to 21.

E X E R C I S E   1

The Right Angle

This is good for people with a round-shouldered back. It looks simple but it is an extremely taxing manoeuvre.

1 Find a clear space of wall with some uncluttered floor in front of it. Sit sideways in to the wall with your bottom as near in to the wall as you can get it.

2 Roll on to your back and swing your legs up against the wall. Stretch your arms out along the floor above your head. You should find yourself in a right-angled bend at the hips.

3 Do not allow your knees to bend or your bottom to lift off the floor. Remain in this position for 2 to 5 minutes.

4 You can make this exercise more taxing by interlacing your fingers and turning them palm-up above your head without bending the elbows.

5 To release from the exercise, bend your legs on the wall, and round your back. With your knees bent, tip on to your side on the floor. NB The longer you have been in the position, the more cast you feel on release. Make small wriggling movements on your side to soften your spine.

177

E X E R C I S E   2

The Floor Twist

1 Sit on the floor with both legs stretched out in front of you.

2 Place your right leg over your left knee and allow your right foot to rest on the floor on the outside of your left knee.

3 Turning your trunk to the left, push your right elbow against the inside of your right knee which levers you further to the left.

4 Hold the position for 30 seconds and then release and relax before repeating twice.

5 Repeat three times in the opposite direction.

EXERCISE 3

The BackBlock

1   Lie on the floor on your back with your knees bent.

2   Lift your bottom off the floor and slide the BackBlock (see page 39) under your bottom. Make sure you don't put it too high up the spine: it should *not* rest under the vertebrae themselves but should go under the sacrum, that hard flat bone at the bottom of the spine.

3   When the BackBlock is in position lower your bottom down on to it and then gradually straighten your legs out along the floor.

4   Relax in this position over the BackBlock. Depending on your degree of 'kink' both at the front of your hips and at your low back, you will feel a pulling sensation in your low back, almost as though your legs are pulling the pelvis off the base of the spine. It should feel agreeably uncomfortable but it may sometimes be difficult to maintain for more than a few seconds if the sense of pulling is too great. It should not be agony although it should feel as if it means business; as if it goes straight to the nub of things.

5   After 30 seconds, or more if you can tolerate it, bend your knees up again, lift your bottom and slide the BackBlock out. Lower your bottom on the floor. It always hurts to raise your bottom off the BackBlock. Don't be fazed by this: the longer you have been lying there, the more it will hurt.

6   Always proceed to the next exercise, Curl Ups.

EXERCISE 4

Curl Ups

After you use the BackBlock you must always follow with curl ups. These must be done well; if you do them badly they can actually make your condition worse. You should aim to do up to thirty curl ups daily but it is far better to do eight curl ups well than do thirty hastily and badly.

1   Lie on your back on the floor with your knees bent and your feet secured under a sofa or heavy chair. Do not under any circumstances attempt this with straight legs.

2   Slowly curl your spine up, bringing your nose towards your knees. Do this vertebra by vertebra until you reach the sitting position. Do not put your hands behind the head because this will encourage you to jerk which will impact the base of the spine.

3   Gently return to the floor by rolling your hips back and pressing your low back into the floor.

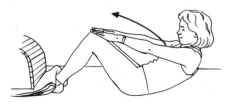

4   Up to thirty curl ups are to be done daily.

The longer you spend on the Back-

Block the more curl ups you have to do. However, it is not ideal to spend long periods (ten to thirty minutes) on the BackBlock. It is better to break it up into shorter periods of one to two minutes each time, followed by the curl ups, say eight to ten each time.

EXERCISE 5

The Plough

This is good for people with a too-straight back. By bearing weight on the shoulders and the upper ribs this exercise gently forces the thoracic spine into a hoop, with a splaying-out effect of the 'fish scales' of the thoracic vertebrae. You will need a robust pillow and a small stool.

1   Position the stool about forty-five centimetres (eighteen inches) away from the pillow on the floor.

2   Lie on your back on the floor with the pillow positioned crossways under your shoulders and your head free on the floor.

3   Raise both legs up and swing them up and over your head so that your feet rest on the stool behind your head. Make this movement smooth not jerky. Support your bottom with your hands (arms bent at the elbow) and hold this position for as long as you can – up to 5 minutes if possible – relaxed and

breathing evenly all the time. The pillow should be positioned to allow a step-down at the point where the thorax becomes the neck and this spares the neck from too much pushing under. The more uncomfortable the neck feels, the higher the pillow step-down should be. You will find the exercise hard to do at first; a pull on the neck and hard to breathe, but even holding it for 15

179

seconds helps. You will feel a mixed sensation of stretch and pain in your middle back which will be relieved only by relaxing into the pain and gently breathing through it.

4   As you practise this you will find that you can progress the movement further by removing the stool and allowing your knees to bend down on to your forehead. Because your head is lower than your heart and because your shoulder girdle is being moved away from the head, this is one of the most relaxing positions for meditation.

EXERCISE 6

The Shoulder Hang

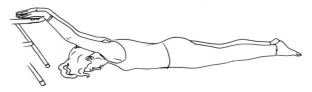

You will need a kitchen chair for this.
1 Lie face down on the floor with the kitchen chair about twenty centimetres (eight inches) beyond your head.
2 Lift one arm at a time and place the flat of each hand on the seat of the chair. (You may have to push the chair further away if you find that the front edge is digging into your forearms.)
3 Straighten both arms at the elbows and drop your head through your shoulders and down towards the floor. You will feel the pull diagonally up under the chest across to the front of the shoulders.
4 Hang there for 1 minute and rest for a while before repeating once.

EXERCISE 7

The Forearm Twist

You will need a kitchen chair for this exercise.
1 Sit comfortably on the chair, extend both arms straight out horizontally in front of you with your hands back to back.
2 Bring your right hand over your left hand so that the palms are facing. Interlace your fingers right down to the web.
3 Keeping your hands locked together bring them down and towards you, in and under through to the chest and then up and out through the space between your arms and stretch them out horizontally again. You will find that this causes an extreme twisting stretch to the forearms and that your fingers will want to disengage.
4 Hold the hands tight and try to straighten your elbows as far as possible. Hold this position for 30 seconds and then gently release.
5 Repeat three times.
6 Change sides bringing the left hand over the right and repeat four times.

EXERCISE 8

The Up-and-Down Hip Stretch

1 Kneel on the floor in front of a kitchen chair.

2 Grasp the back of the chair to keep stable and keeping your left knee on the floor, lift your right foot up on to the chairseat. If this is too difficult start from the opposite direction: stand in front of the chair, lift your right foot on to the seat, then sink down on to your left knee on the floor. Whichever way you approach this, don't let your hips kink and your bottom poke out and try to keep your back straight. If both these methods are too difficult you may need to start with a lower chair.

3 Hold the position for 1 minute and release.

4 Repeat with the other leg.

5 Repeat the sequence two more times for each leg.

EXERCISE 9

The Sitting Bowl

1 Kneel on the floor.

2 Keeping your knees and your big toes pressed together, hook your thumbs around the inner side of each heel and pull them outwards.

3 With the heels as widely separated as possible, lower your bottom down into the bowl-shaped hollow made by your feet.

4 Sit there for 40 seconds with your bottom pressing your heels apart.

5 Release and relax and then repeat once more.

EXERCISE 10

The Toes Push-Back

1 Kneel on the floor on your hands and knees.

2 Lean forwards on your hands and turn the tops of your toes under so that the toe-pads are on the floor.

3 Sit back on the turned-under toes for 30 seconds.

4 Release and repeat the sequence three times.

INDEX

abdominal muscles, 27–8
accessory movements,
    11–15
    ankles, 153–4
    elbows, 98–9
    feet, 168–9
    knees, 135–6
    lumbar spine, 28–9
    neck, 64–6
    shoulders, 81–3
    thoracic spine, 48–50
    wrists, 107
acetabulum, 116
Achilles stretch, 161
acromio-clavicular
    joint, 78
acute locked back, 35–6
acute neck, 68–9
aerobics, 17–18
ageing, 12–13
ankles, 14–15, 148–63
    accessory
        movements, 153–4
    anatomy, 148–50
    exercises, 160–3
    functions, 150–3
    problems, 154–60

ankles-touching
    tiptoes, 163
'antalgic' positions, 71
anxiety, neck pain, 73
arches, feet, 149–57, 168–9,
    170–2
arching the foot exercise,
    174
arms: brachial neuralgia,
    70–1
    'dead arm' syndrome, 53
    elbows, 95–103
    muscles, 50, 81–3
    and shoulders, 78–94
    thoracic kyphosis, 52
    weakness, 84
    wrists, 104–15
arthritis: hips, 122–7
    knees, 138–40
    neck, 71–3
    spine, 33–5
arthroscopy, 138
articular disc, 106
atlas vertebra, 62
autonomic nervous system,
    53
axis vertebra, 63

back see low back; thoracic
    spine
backache, 34
BackBlock, 39, 40, 59–60, 178
backwards arch, 44
backwards shoulder, 90–1
behind your back twist, 93
bow-legs, 142
brachial neuralgia, 70–1
breathing, 21, 46–7
broken bones, 109–10
broomstick stretch, 94
bunions, 172–4
buttock stretch, 127

calcaneum, 149–50, 152, 153,
    164
calf muscle, 66–7, 166–7
calluses, feet, 170, 172, 173
carpal bones, 105–7, 113
cartilage: hips, 116, 123–4
    knees, 131, 134, 136,
        137–8, 140
cervical spondylosis, 69, 71–3
child's squat, 146
chondromalacia patella,
    141–3

chronically twisting ankle, 157–60
clavicle, 78
Colles fracture, 110
condyles, femoral, 132–3, 134, 137, 144
cortisone, 102
costo-vertebral joints, 48–9, 53
crepitus, 139
crossed-sole stretch, 161–2
cruciate ligaments, 134
curl ups, 41, 178–9

daily regime, 177–81
'dead-arm' syndrome, 53
dead blow fly exercise, 128
deltoid muscle, 81
discs: lumbar vertebrae, 24–5, 26, 30–9
neck vertebrae, 62, 70
dislocation, shoulders, 81
dowling torture exercise, 176

elbow lift, 74
elbows, 95–103
accessory movements, 98–9
anatomy, 95
exercises, 102–3
functions, 95–8
problems, 99–101
emotions, neck pain, 73

face pain, 72
facet joints: lumbar vertebrae, 25, 27, 32, 34–7
neck vertebrae, 62, 64, 65–6, 68, 70, 71
fallen arches, 170–2
feet, 164–76
accessory movements, 168–9
anatomy, 164–5
ankles, 148–63
exercises, 174–6
functions, 166–8
problems, 169–74
sagging inner arches, 156–7
femoral condyles, 132–3, 134, 137, 144

femur, 116–21, 126, 131, 132–4
fibula, 131, 148–9, 156
fingers, 105, 106
flat feet, 170–2
floor lunge, 129–30
floor twist, 58, 177
foot squash, 160
foot twist, 162
forearm stretch, 102–3
forearm twist, 103, 180
forwards bend, 42
fractures, 109–10
frozen shoulder, 86–7

glenoid cavity, 79, 83
golf, 8

hamstrings, 81
hands: elbows and, 95–8
wrists, 104–15
head: neck muscles, 67
neck vertebrae, 62–3
thoracic kyphosis, 51
head clasp, 74
headaches, 72, 118
heel bone see calcaneum
herniated lumbar discs, 38–9
hips, 116–30
accessory movements, 120–1
anatomy, 116–18
exercises, 127–30
functions, 118–20
problems, 121–6
'turn out', 171
humerus, 78–81, 89
hyaline cartilage, 123–4

ilio-femoral ligament, 120
impaction, spine, 29–30, 39
in-toeing, 171
inflammation, 68–9
interlaced finger stretch, 114

joints: accessory movements, 11–15
misuse, 6–10
see also individual joints
joints of Luschka, 62

knee bounce, 40–1
knee clenches, 145

knee seesaw, 145–6
knee swings, 144–5
kneecap (patella), 131–2, 136
irritation of, 141–3
kneeling rock, 114
knees, 9, 131–47
accessory movements, 12, 135–6
anatomy, 131–4
exercises, 144–7
functions, 134–5
problems, 136–43
knees apart stretch, 128
knock-knees, 142, 171
kyphosis, thoracic, 51–2

legs: ankles, 148–63
hips, 116–30
knees, 131–47
muscles, 66–7, 81, 166–7
ligaments: knees, 133–4
spinal, 27
locking mechanism, knees, 134–5, 136, 137
low back, 22–44
accessory movements, 28–9
anatomy, 22–6
exercises, 40–4
functions, 26–8
problems, 29–39
lumbago, 33–5
lumbar spine see low back
lumbar spondylosis, 33–5
lunate, 107–8, 109

menisci, 134
metacarpal bones, 105
metatarsal bones, 150, 152, 154, 164–5, 170, 172–3
migraine, 72, 118
muscles: ankles, 150–3
calf, 66–7, 166–7
elbow, 99–100
knees, 131–2, 137–8
and loss of accessory joint movement, 13–15
neck, 63–4, 66–8, 72–3
protective spasm, 14–15, 158
quadriceps, 81, 131–2, 143

183

movement—*contd*
scapula, 83–5
shoulders, 80–3, 85–8
toes, 166, 167, 169, 172
wrists, 99, 111–12
navicular bone, 149–50, 151, 152
neck, 61–77
accessory movements, 64–6
anatomy, 61–3
disorders, 68–73
exercises, 74–7
functions, 63–4
problems, 66–8
nerves: autonomic nervous system, 53
brachial neuralgia, 70–1
sciatica, 26, 35, 36, 37–8
neuralgia, brachial, 70–1

orthotics, 157
osteoarthritis, hips, 122–7

palm, 105
patella *see* kneecap
pectoral muscles, 52
pelvic slant, 43
pelvis: and ankle in-rolling, 157
hips, 116–30
peroneus brevis, 155
peroneus longus, 166–7, 171–2
phasic muscles, 83–4, 111–12
pigeon toes, 171–2
plough, 58–9, 75, 179
postural muscles, 111
praying shoulder stretch, 91
protective muscle spasm, 158

quadriceps muscles, 81, 131–2, 143
quadriceps tendon, 131–2, 142

radius, 95, 96–98, 104, 106, 110
referred pain, 72
reflexology, 173–4
repetitive strain injury (RSI), 110–13
retinaculum, 112
reverse prayer, 115

'reverse scapulo-humeral rhythm', 84
ribs, 45–50
right angle exercise, 55–6, 177
rolling pin stretch, 92–3
rotator cuff muscles, 81, 83

sacrum, 22
scaphoid, 108, 110
scapula, 79–81, 83–5
scar tissue, 158
sciatic stretch, 44
sciatica, 26, 35, 36, 37–8
scoliosis, 51, 54
self-traction twist, 42–3
sergeant-major's back, 52–3
shear, 28–9
shin-bone *see* tibia
shoes, 169, 170, 171, 172–3, 174
shoulder hang, 90, 180
shoulders, 78–94
accessory movements, 81–3
anatomy, 78–9
exercises, 90–4
functions, 79–81
problems, 83–9
sitting, 30–1
sitting bowl, 147, 181
skull, vertebrae, 62–3
spine: lumbar spine, 22–44
thoracic spine, 45–60
spondylolisthesis, 33
spondylosis, cervical, 69, 71–3
sprained wrists, 109–10
spring ligament, 152–3, 155
steroids, 102
supraspinatus muscle, 88
swastika, 76
swimming, 88
synovial fluid, 123–5, 140
synovium, knees, 139–40

'T' shape, 92
talus, 148–9, 150, 153–5
tarsal bones, 148, 164
tendonitis, 82, 88–9
tendons, wrists, 112–13
tennis, 8, 52
tennis ball release, 60
tennis elbow, 101–2

tension, neck pain, 73
30 minute daily regime, 177–81
thoracic arms tangle, 56
thoracic kyphosis, 51–2
thoracic side bend, 57
thoracic spine, 45–60
accessory movements, 48–50
anatomy, 45–7
disorders, 51–4
exercises, 55–60
functions, 47–8
problems, 50–1
thumbs, 106, 107
tibia, 131, 132–4, 148–9
tibialis anterior, 151–2, 155
tibialis posterior, 152, 155, 166–7
tipped head and neck twist, 77
toes, 150, 164–7, 169–74
toes push-back, 175, 181
toes push-under, 175
trabeculae, 24, 117–18
trapezius muscle, 69
twist on all fours, 57
twisted ankles, 157–60

ulna, 95, 96–8, 104, 106
up-and-down hip stretch, 129, 181

vastus medialis, 137–8
vertebrae: lumbar, 22–44
neck, 61–77
thoracic, 45–60

walking, 118–20, 121, 126, 135, 167, 168
whiplash injuries, 68
wrists, 104–15
accessory movements, 11–12, 107
anatomy, 104–6
exercises, 114–15
functions, 106–7
muscles, 99
problems, 107–13
writing, 99

yoga, 16–19